LiTTLE GUiDES

Dog Care

LiTTLE GUiDES

Dog Care

FOG CITY PRESS

Published by Fog City Press
814 Montgomery Street
San Francisco, CA 94133 USA

Copyright © 2005 Weldon Owen Pty Ltd
First printed 2005

ISBN 1 740893 49 2

Color reproduction by SC (Sang Choy) International Pte Ltd
Printed by SNP Leefung Printers Ltd
Printed in China

A Weldon Owen Production
Produced using arkiva retrieval technology
For further information, contact
arkiva@weldonowen.com.au

FOG CITY PRESS
Chief Executive Officer: John Owen
President: Terry Newell
Publisher: Sheena Coupe
Creative Director: Sue Burk
Project Manager: Jessica Cox
Editorial Coordinators: Helen Flint, Irene Mickaiel
Production Manager: Louise Mitchell
Production Coordinator: Monique Layt
Sales Manager: Emily Jahn
Vice President International Sales: Stuart Laurence

Consulting Editor: Dr. Paul McGreevy

Project Editor: Helen Bateman
Project Designer: Lena Lowe

Contents

All about dogs

GETTING A DOG

WHETHER IT COMES WITH A PEDIGREE OR
FROM A POUND, A DOG IS JUST ABOUT THE
PERFECT FRIEND. THE RESPONSIBILITIES OF
OWNERSHIP ARE GREAT, BUT THE LOVE AND
FRIENDSHIP YOU WILL RECEIVE ARE PRICELESS.

12 | Choosing the right dog

The bond between you and your dog can be very rewarding, and to give this relationship the best chance of success, choose your pet carefully. Consider your lifestyle, your home, your family needs—and what your dog will need from you. Consider the cost of owning a dog, taking into account food, equipment, and veterinary care. Learn as much as you can about the characteristics of the different breeds, and the differences in temperament between the sexes, so you can choose the dog that best suits you and your family.

Playful pugs
Pugs make an ideal pet, especially if space is limited. They love company and are good with children.

Growing up together
While dogs can make
great companions for
children, do not forget
that you are ultimately
responsible for them.

Puppy or older dog?

Puppies and adult dogs have different needs and make different demands of their owners. If you get a puppy, you can train it how you want, because you will have more control over its learning during its first crucial months of life. However, a puppy will demand a lot of your time and patience in both supervision and training. An older dog will be better at keeping itself entertained, and will need less supervision. With an older dog, find out as much as you can about its history. It may well have behavioral problems that might not be obvious.

Why a puppy?
- Easier to train
- Grows up with family
- Bonds more quickly

Why an older dog?
- Demands less attention
- Already house-trained
- Needs less training

Mother's influence
A puppy's mother will teach it vital lessons about how to behave, which means less work for you, its new owner.

16 | A healthy pup

Early influence
Choose your pup from an alert, active, and well-fed litter, like these Cavalier King Charles spaniels. Observe the mother's behavior as a guide.

Make sure you choose a pup that is going to be fit and healthy. While there is no guarantee that your new puppy will never fall ill, you can reduce the chances by checking for certain signs when making your choice. Watch how the puppies interact with each other. Avoid the most bossy and shy pups. Make sure your pup's parents have been checked for any genetic health problems, and consult your vet for information about disorders that are specific to the breed.

Nose
Usually cold and wet, but not running

Eyes
Clear, bright, and expressive, free of discharge, not red

Body
Strong and symmetrical (i.e. no signs of poor growth)

Ears
Clean, free of discharge, not red or odorous

Skin
Under the coat: not oily, no flakes or dandruff, no scabs or lumps

Mouth
Gums pink, teeth white, pleasant-smelling "puppy breath"

Anus
Clean and dry, not red or irritated

Legs
Walks and runs effortlessly, puts even weight on all legs

Belly
Often free of hair, pink, no sores or pimples

Fur
Clean and shiny, little or no shedding when stroked, no fleas or flea dirt

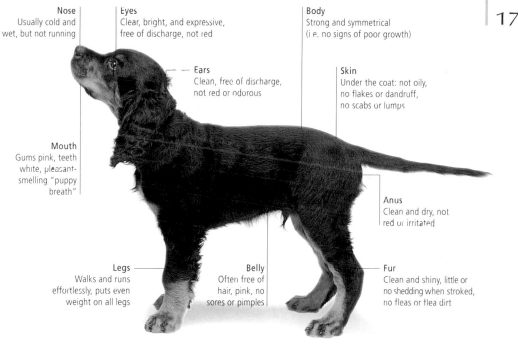

18 Purebred dogs

Purebred dogs tend to have distinct appearances and are genetically predisposed to behave in certain, predictable ways. This means that when you decide on a purebred, you will have a good idea of the looks, character, eventual size, and behavior of the dog you are getting. Purebred dogs are classified according to the breed's original purpose. It is a good idea to get advice from impartial experts when looking for a dog that suits you best. Be aware that breeds are created from a smaller gene pool, which means that a purebred dog's inherited predisposition to certain illnesses is increased.

Health problem
Scottish terriers can inherit a blood-clotting disorder called von Willebrand's disease.

Breed differences
Golden retrievers need more
exercise and grooming than
Pembroke Welsh corgis. Both
breeds are easy to train, have
cheerful temperaments, and
make good pets for kids.

Mixed breed dogs

The mixed breed, or mutt, is the ordinary, sometimes quirky-looking, everyday kind of dog. Your mixed breed dog will make a devoted companion, and it can be trained to behave as well as any purebred. Many people believe that mixed breeds are hardier and healthier than purebreds because the genetic mix lessens the likelihood of it developing hereditary illnesses. But it can still get sick from non-hereditary illnesses. Choose your dog because you like its personality and looks, and remember that mixed in any dog's genetic pool is an assortment of genes—the good and the not-so-good.

A good companion
Regardless of its pedigree, this German shepherd mix needs to be loved, valued, and cared for in the same way as a purebred.

A happy mix
It may not win any ribbons, but this poodle-terrier mix will win plenty of hearts.

22 | Where to get a dog

Once you have decided what sort of dog you want, you have to decide where to acquire it. A purebred dog can be very expensive, but if you go to a reputable, knowledgeable breeder, you will get your money's worth. Avoid backyard breeders who breed their dogs and sell their puppies as a way of making money. Their dogs will not always meet the breed standard. Breed rescue organizations take in unwanted purebreds and help them find new homes. The best place to find a mixed breed is at an animal shelter. Talk to your vet to find out which are well-organized and run by trained staff.

Good home wanted
Fine dogs can often be found in dog shelters and breed rescue groups. Make sure you know what kind of dog you want before you go.

Good breeders
Reputable breeders, like the breeder of these West Highland white terriers, screen any potential buyers.

24 | Preparing for a new dog

Your new dog will be eager to explore—and taste—its new surroundings. Before your dog moves in, make sure your home is safe for it. Keep garbage safely stored away. An elevated shower caddy will keep soaps, shampoos, and conditioners out of harm's way. Keep medications out of reach, and secure your chocolate—it can make your dog seriously ill. If you have a yard, check that the fencing is secure, that there are no holes, and that the gates shut firmly. Take care to remove any toxic plants from the garden.

A cozy home
Very large breeds, such as these Newfoundlands, may be more comfortable outside in a kennel than inside the house.

A nose for trouble

Dogs are constantly using their nose and mouth to explore the world around them. They also have surprisingly agile paws, so it is important to store cleaning supplies and solvents where they can do no harm.

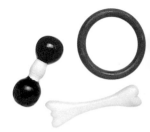

Designer bowls

Stainless steel or ceramic bowls (below) are more durable and hygienic than plastic ones. Solid rubber or nylon chew toys (top right) ease teething pains and save your belongings.

There are a few essential items you need that will make life easier for you and will keep your dog happy and healthy. The first thing that your dog will need is a warm, clean, comfortable bed. There is a range of collars and a variety of leashes available. Choose carefully. Check your pup's collar each week to make sure it has not become too tight. If your dog needs a muzzle, get one that allows it to pant and drink water, but not to bite.

After the event

Pooper-scoopers come in many varieties and are available at pet supply stores.

Canine couture
Pet supply stores sell a variety of jackets, rain slickers, and cordura-soled booties that keep your dog warm, dry, and protected in rugged terrain.

28 | Settling in

Old friends
Dogs and cats are not natural enemies and will usually get on very well if encouraged to respect each other.

When you first bring your new dog home, it will probably be confused and apprehensive, so let it settle in gently. Spend some time with your dog to get it used to you and the other members of its new family "pack." Restrict your pup to one room and let it familiarize itself with its surroundings. If it seems homesick, give it a toy or blanket that carries the smell of its old family to comfort it. Bringing a puppy's bed and crate into your bedroom at night may help it to settle in.

Getting acquainted
Dogs, such as this border
collie, should be introduced
to children gradually and
under adult supervision.

Tips for settling in
- Be gentle
- Let your pup sniff around
- Introduce it to other pets
  and family members
- Show food and water bowls

30 Puppies' special needs

Your new pup needs special care. Pups learn by repetition and consistency, so establish a routine that will help your pup make sense of its home and what you want from it. Until your pup is about four or five months of age, feed it three times a day. Begin house-training. Be patient and persistent and your pup should be house-trained by three or four months old. Play, with you and with other dogs, is also necessary for your pup's social development.

Nap time
For the first few weeks of life, puppies spend much of their time sleeping.

A formative time
Positive situations, sensations, and experiences are crucial for socializing a new puppy.

Responsible dog ownership

Along with the pleasures of owning a dog come various legal and social obligations. Laws regarding dog ownership vary from place to place. It is common for owners to be required to keep their dogs leashed in public places, and certain breeds may also be required to wear muzzles. Most countries require that dogs be licensed or registered, and be able to be identified either by a tag, microchip, or tattoo. Familiarize yourself with any local laws. Train your dog to be well-behaved around people, and if you are not planning to breed professionally, it is responsible to neuter your dog.

Safety first
Some dogs need to wear a muzzle for public safety or for grooming purposes. Leather muzzles (below left) and nylon muzzles (below right) are readily available from pet supply stores.

Cleaning up its act
Always clean up after your dog in a public place, for the sake of other people.

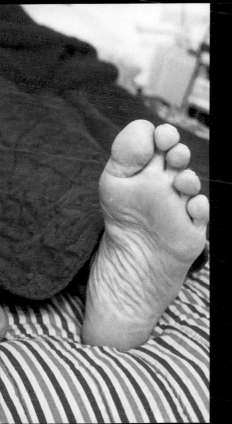

UNDERSTANDING
DOGS

YOUR DOG HAS WAYS OF HEARING, SEEING,
AND THINKING THAT ARE DIFFERENT TO
YOURS, AND THIS CAN LEAD TO CONFUSION.
FINDING A WAY TO "TALK" TO EACH OTHER
IS THE KEY TO A HAPPY LIFE TOGETHER.

36 | Pack animals

Pack leader
Dogs, such as this boxer, look up to their leader for guidance and reassurance.

In the dog world, you are either a leader or a follower. It does not matter how many people or other animals there are in its family, your dog's instinct is to find out where it stands. Most dogs are born followers, but if you do not take the role of leader, your dog will fill the vacancy. Without using force, you can steer its pack behavior in a positive direction. Act like the wolf leader who controls the food, and feed your dog when you have finished eating. Wait until your dog is sitting quietly before you attach the leash and take it for a walk. This way, your dog will always know where it stands.

Choice location

Comfort is not the only reason
dogs take over the furniture.
In the wild, high sleeping
grounds were always taken
by the pack leader. Getting
your dog off the furniture
will reinforce your dog's
subordinate position in
the family pack.

How dogs communicate

Dogs are expert communicators who use an elaborate repertoire of body postures, sounds, and scent to get their message across. When dogs meet, they first establish rank by positioning themselves to sniff each other's anal sacs. This interaction tells them the sex, status, age, and attitude of the other. Dogs use their body to express affection, assert possession, or impose rank. As a general rule, submissive dogs shrink down, while dominant dogs puff up. Barks, whines, and growls all have a place in canine language.

Using scent

After anal sniffing has been conducted, the sniffer may sniff the new dog's nose and lips. For dogs that know each other, such as these Cavalier King Charles spaniel siblings, this sniffing is more common.

Friends and equals

With their extroverted body language—direct eye contact, loosely open mouths, and confident body positions— these dogs indicate they are comfortable with one another.

Using sound

Bred to bark
Jack Russell terriers were bred
to kill vermin and, to an extent,
to alert their owners to the
presence of prey by barking.

Your dog is capable of a variety of noises—barks, growls,
whines, yelps, and howls—that can mean different things
at different times. Although barking may seem the simplest
method of canine communication, the bark's context adds
an important layer of complexity. Barking can mean that
your dog is having fun, is feeling frightened or lonely, wants
attention, or hears a noise. It could also be warning you of
a stranger approaching. In general, the faster and higher the
bark, the more excited or agitated the dog; but sometimes
dogs just bark out of habit. Growling is a warning sound.
Dogs that growl and look submissive are usually frightened.

A good howl
Like their wolf ancestors, dogs howl to communicate over long distances. Some dogs have different howls for different situations.

Is it playtime yet?
With its front end down,
its rear end up, and its tail
wagging furiously, this
whippet mix is telling its
owner it is ready to play.

Reading a dog's reactions | 43

Dogs express themselves using their body positions, facial expressions, ear and tail movements, and a variety of sounds. If your dog's ears are pulled down and back, it is probably feeling frightened or submissive. If they are pricked, it is stimulated by something, and may even be aggressive. A wagging tail usually indicates a friendly dog, but it also could mean that it is scared or agitated. Mounting and humping are sometimes expressions of dominance, while tongue-flicking usually means your dog is tense or concentrating. Watch your dog and you will soon work out its particular body language.

Common reactions
- Ears down
- Ears pricked
- Tail-wagging
- Mounting and humping
- Tongue-flicking

Feeling insecure
This cattle dog signals its uncertainty with an anxious, pleading look and by holding its ears at different angles.

44 | Communicating with a dog

Just as your dog's body language indicates its moods and reactions, your body, face, and voice are sending signals to your dog. You need to send your dog signals it can recognize. Except for a few vocal commands they understand, dogs mainly respond to intonations and body language. Too much exuberance can send the dog wrong signals and your dog may become anxious. But gestures such as opening your arms are positive signals. Adopt a confident posture and an enthusiastic attitude and your dog will obey your commands.

All in the tone
This boxer knows that its owner's serious tone means a reprimand.

Love to spare
Improving your relationship through better communication will have long-term benefits.

TRAINING YOUR DOG

EVERY DOG NEEDS TO BE TAUGHT BASIC
GOOD MANNERS. A CRITICAL GOAL OF
TRAINING IS TO HELP YOUR DOG RECOGNIZE
YOU AS ITS LEADER. YOU MUST BE FIRM AND
DECISIVE IN SETTING THE BOUNDARIES.

Watch me
1 With your dog facing you, point to your eyes and say "watch me." Maintain eye contact for about 10 seconds.

2 Release your dog and say "good dog!" Repeat frequently at various locations.

It is never too early to start training. Keep sessions short, but do not confine training to specific times. Incorporate exercises into your daily routine so that your dog can practice what it has learned. Some dogs learn commands in hours, while others may take weeks. A daily routine builds good learning habits. Choose a quiet area at first, with few distractions or interruptions, then graduate to somewhere more challenging.

Start young
This pup is learning good manners while it is young— the best time for learning.

52 | Training tips

The power of rewards
Reward your dog with snacks, pats, and plenty of praise. You will find that its good behavior will increase only if it is followed by a reward.

As leader, you need to set firm rules about what it is you want from your dog. Give consistent commands, in the same tone of voice, and in the same order. Never hit or shout at your dog. Harsh correction can result in fear and aggression, both of which will hinder learning. Reprimand your dog immediately or it will not know why it is being reprimanded.

Positive reinforcement
Never let good behavior go unnoticed. Your dog knows that behaving well makes good things happen, and therefore makes it happy.

54 Leashes and collars

Before leash-training your dog, make sure it has a comfortable collar. A good first collar is a nylon, leather buckle, or snap-on collar. It should fit snugly around the neck. Although now falling out of favor, choke chains and pinch collars are still sometimes used for training. They should be used only by experienced owners.

Choke chains
When put on backward (top) a choke chain will not loosen and could suffocate your dog. Check the ring end attached to the leash comes over the neck (bottom) and the chain will be able to loosen.

Match size and shape
Do not weigh a small dog
down with a heavy, leather
collar Check out the variety
below: (from top) a rolled
collar; three leather collars;
and a nylon snap-on collar.

Getting used to a leash

Every dog reacts differently when it hears the click of a leash and feels the tug on its collar. If you train your dog correctly, you will soon have it walking politely on a leash. Have your puppy drag the leash around the house for short periods. Start by putting on your dog's training collar, then attach the leash to this. Do not tug your dog. Gradually coax it to move with you. If its concentration wanders, give a quick pull on the leash. Your dog will soon understand that whenever you put the leash on it, you want it to pay attention to you.

Follow the leader
A dog that knows how to walk by its owner's side, like this Shiba Inu, is a pleasure to walk.

Who is walking whom?
A dog that pulls constantly on the leash can turn an enjoyable stroll into a shoulder-wrenching marathon.

58 | Teaching "Sit"

The fact that a dog has a relatively inflexible spine means that if it tips its head up far enough, it will sit. You can use this to your advantage when teaching a dog to sit in response to a spoken command. By raising a food treat, you can easily get

1 With your dog facing you, hold a food reward between your fingers and thumb, with your palm face up, in front of its nose.

2 Move the reward up and slightly back over your dog's head. Say "sit" once as you do this. As your dog follows the treat with its eyes and head, it will sit down.

your dog to sit. Repeat the process below six to eight times, praising it each time. Only say the word "sit" once as you maneuver the puppy into a sit. Be careful not to hold the food too high above the dog's nose as it might jump up to reach it.

Family help
Enlist the assistance of all the family and your dog will soon learn to sit on command.

3 Praise your dog, saying "good sit," and give it the food reward.

60 | Teaching "Down"

Use food to help guide your dog into position when you want to teach it to lie down. Follow the steps below, and if you find that your dog will not go into position, you can try pushing the treat between its front legs. As it tries to follow the treat, its back end will slide into a down position.

1 Place your dog in a sit. Hold a food treat in front of it, say "down," and quickly bring the food down to the ground so its head follows.

2 If your dog needs help, gently guide its shoulders downward. When your dog is lying down, praise it, and give it the treat.

Getting the message
Once your dog associates the word "down" with the action you can be less reliable with the food treats—but keep praising it each time it obeys.

62 | Teaching "Come"

Teaching a dog to come is an extremely important and often difficult task. Never call your dog to you and punish it. Take care not to call it away from something fun. Practice calling your dog and when it comes, praise it and send it back to play.

1 Stand close to your dog with a food reward in your hand.

2 Back up a short distance, wiggle the treat and say "come."

A warm welcome
Eventually, your "come" command can be paired with welcoming body language to encourage a positive response.

3 As your dog approaches, say "good come," and give it a treat when it gets to you.

Well trained

Teaching "stay" can be a difficult task, but it is important that your dog will stay reliably when told.

1 With your dog in sit, place your hand, palm open, in front of its face.

Teaching "Stay"

Teaching your dog to stay on command may avoid a disaster,
especially if you live in a busy urban area. Aim for small
successes, not long stays. At first, reward a stay of five
seconds, then gradually increase the duration of the stay.

2 Slowly walk backward
from your dog, all the
while making eye contact
and telling it to "stay."

3 If your puppy does not
move for five seconds, go
back and reward it with
food and praise.

66 Teaching "Heel"

There are two ways to teach your dog to heel. The first is an extension of the "watch me" command (see page 50). Repeat this command several times and add the command "heel." At first move only short distances, but gradually move farther

1 Have your dog on a leash at your left side. Hold the leash with your right hand so that it crosses your body. Keep your right hand at your waist.

2 As you start walking, say your dog's name and "heel." If necessary, hold on the leash with your left hand until the dog is beside you, then release.

and for longer periods as your dog learns to stay with you. The second method of teaching the "heel" command is outlined in the steps below. This exercise cannot be practiced easily inside. Be prepared to spend a lot of time outdoors.

3 If your dog starts to pull or lag, turn in the opposite direction. Do not worry if you collide. It will soon realize it should be watching you.

4 When your dog is walking nicely by your side, praise it verbally, saying "good heel." You can also reach down and pet it.

68 | House-training puppies

Just in case
These young Australian shepherds are confined to a crate when they cannot be supervised indoors.

A good house-training routine for your puppy should be established from the first day you bring it home. Your puppy is most likely to eliminate within 10 minutes of eating, or immediately after waking or playing. Your house-training will be most successful if you take your dog outside at these times. Praise any successes. If you catch your dog in the act inside, distract it, tell it "outside," and quickly take it outside.

An indoor option
This boxer pup is being trained to urinate on newspapers if left indoors.

70 | Getting used to travel

Home away from home
A traveling crate is a good investment, especially if you have a puppy. Buy one large enough to accommodate your pup when it is fully grown.

If you are planning a car trip with your dog, prepare your pet well in advance for its time in the car, and the new sights and sounds it will encounter. Let your dog explore the car and then take it for a short drive around the block. Dogs can suffer from anxiety and motion sickness, just like humans. Place a plastic tablecloth on the back seat to protect the car's interior. Once it is happy to undertake longer journeys, remember to stop every few hours to allow your dog to stretch its legs and relieve itself.

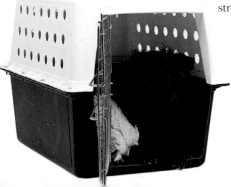

Time to go!
Dog car seat harnesses (left),
crates, and barriers are
available at pet supply stores.
They will prevent your dog
from disturbing you while
you are driving.

Traveling tips
• Prepare your dog
• Dog-proof your car
• Stop for breaks

BEHAVIOR PROBLEMS

RECOGNIZE WHAT IS CAUSING YOUR DOG
TO MISBEHAVE, AND A SOLUTION WILL NOT
BE DIFFICULT TO FIND. HOWEVER, THE BEST
WAY TO STOP BAD BEHAVIOR IS TO PREVENT
IT FROM GETTING STARTED.

Looking for trouble
Certain breeds, including Jack Russells and some other terriers, can be aggressive around other dogs.

For dogs, aggression is just another form of communication, like wagging their tail. It is a dog's way of setting boundaries. However, it is a potentially dangerous problem that needs to be stopped quickly before it escalates. Aggression includes growling, barking, snarling, lunging, snapping, and biting. The best way to deal with aggressive behavior is to establish yourself as leader from the outset. Socialize your pup early to prevent it from feeling insecure, and avoid playing competitive games, such as tug-of-war. Exercise and obedience training can help, but keep your dog leashed in public places.

Bred for fighting
Some breeds, such as American Staffordshire terriers, have been bred for their aggression.

76 | Barking

A dog barks to communicate, to indicate excitement or fear, or to warn of intruders. But barking can be annoying for owners and neighbors alike. If you have a dog that barks to excess, it is important to determine the motivation. If your dog is lonely, it may be comforted by the sound of a radio or television. If it is bored, a puzzle game may entertain it. If it is frightened by something, try desensitizing it to that stimulus.

A noisy distraction
Most dogs bark for a reason, but some bark out of habit. You can startle your dog into silence by tossing a tin half-filled with nails (right) in its direction.

Teaching "quiet"

1 To train a dog to stop barking, you must first get it to start. Make it bark a few times and tell it "good bark." Do this until it barks on command.

2 Give the command to get it barking. As it pauses between barks, hold a treat over its nose and say "quiet" or "hush," using the same word each time.

3 When it stops barking to sniff the treat, praise it and give it the treat. Keep practicing until it stops barking when you issue the "quiet" command.

78 | Begging

Dogs beg because they want what you are eating. Never give your dog food from the table. If you reward its begging, it will soon progress to drooling, whining, and jumping up on your lap every meal. The extra food will also make your dog gain weight and, since a dog's digestive system is not the same as a human's, it can get sick from eating too much human food.

No more mooching
Train your dog to stop begging by ignoring the behavior. Praise it and offer it a treat when it does not beg.

Dogs get a lot of fun and satisfaction from chewing. It is a natural activity and helps to exercise their jaws and clean their teeth. However, dogs that spend a lot of time alone will sometimes chew as a way of dispelling loneliness, anxiety, frustration, or boredom. Do not try to stop it, just direct the behavior to more appropriate objects, such as chew toys, and find ways to relieve your dog's tension.

Thwarting destruction
If you do not want your dog to chew your new shoes, do not let it chew your old ones. It cannot tell the difference.

Climbing on furniture

At some point, nearly every dog will attempt to stake a claim on the furniture because it is soft and comfortable and allows them to be close to their people. But climbing on the furniture can be an attempt to enhance its status, and with some dogs this may become a problem. To discourage your dog from jumping up on the furniture, lay plastic bubble wrap on top of it. The next time it jumps up it will be startled by the sound and feel. At the same time, provide a comfortable bed right next to the couch (or next to you) or in the center of the room where your dog can see what is going on.

Time's up
Dogs love to climb on furniture. This Australian kelpie mix knows that "off" means it must give up its place on the sofa.

Digging is instinctive in dogs. Most of them love to dig and they do it for many reasons. Some may be bored and want to feel busy, others may dig to escape. In hot weather, some simply may be trying to create a cool place in which to lie. Consider giving your dog its own digging spot in the yard and putting bricks over a non-acceptable area to deter it from digging there. A busy dog is less likely to dig, so take it running with you to burn off excess energy.

A desire to dig
For a dog that loves to dig, such as this Australian shepherd, toys, boots, and anything else it can find may end up in the ground.

82 | Fear

Getting used to it
Some dogs, like this collie-cattle dog mix, are fearful of an everyday object like a vacuum cleaner. You should desensitize the dog to it.

A well-adjusted dog will take unusual situations in its stride; however, some dogs have a difficult time making sense of the world around them. Get your dog used to people, sounds, and situations between 7 and 14 weeks of age. Obedience training will also boost its confidence. Your dog takes its cues from you, so act calm. Rather than comforting it when it is nervous, which may lead it to associate fear with praise, distract it from the source of its fear and praise it when it copes well.

Dislike of handling

Some dogs will take all the attention you can give them; others maintain a strict hands-off policy. Your dog may like to be petted, but will try to wriggle away when you want to groom it, or when your vet wants to examine it. Accustom your pup to your touch from the moment you bring it home. The more you touch it, the more it will trust you. If your dog struggles and bites, verbally rebuke it and praise it when it stops. Forcing it to comply will make it distrustful.

Loving touch
Teach your dog that your hands always have a positive intent—such as petting, feeding, grooming, and comforting.

Jumping up

Many dogs jump up when they are excited and pleased to see you, but others may do it to impose rank. Owners often inadvertently reinforce this behavior by letting their dog jump up in some situations, but not in others. Jumping up often gets attention, even if it is just you pushing it away, and this may encourage your dog to do it again. Ignoring your dog, by turning your back until it obeys the command to sit, is effective. When greeting people, keep your dog on a leash and make it sit before it is greeted. For persistent jumpers, headcollars can be a helpful control.

Glad to see you
When a large dog like this
Newfoundland jumps up, the
effect can be overwhelming.

Dogs tend to be possessive of things they see as valuable resources, such as food or toys. This behavior is a challenge to your leadership, and it can lead to aggression. Possessiveness can be dangerous, especially around small children or other pets. Train your dog to share, even a new toy, by offering another toy or a food treat in exchange. If your dog acts possessively near its feeding bowl or feeding place, put the bowl away after each feed, and vary the places where you feed it.

Come and get it
It is important to teach your dog not to be possessive with playthings, even in a game.

86 | Stealing

Teaching "drop"

1 Get your dog to sit. Give it an object to hold in its mouth. It should be large enough for you to grasp as well.

2 While your dog is holding the object, say "hold" and praise it for a few moments.

3 Take the object from its mouth, pulling the leash downward as you say "drop."

4 Praise your dog when it drops the object. Repeat until it learns to drop it quickly, then test it with other objects.

Some dogs steal to get your attention. Others steal simply because they can. When it comes to food, many dogs cannot resist, no matter how well fed they are. When your puppy begins to steal, never give chase—it will think you are playing a game. Instead, crouch down and ask it to come to you. Then try to take the object while saying "drop"—an important command that should be taught from an early age.

Caught in the act
This vizsla has found a dangerous meal.

EXERCISE

THE KEY TO A HAPPY, HEALTHY DOG—BIG OR
SMALL—IS REGULAR EXERCISE. PET DOGS
TEND TO GET OVERWEIGHT, OUT OF SHAPE,
BORED, AND LAZY. ALWAYS MAKE THE
TIME TO EXERCISE YOUR PET.

Regular exercise
These border collies must get plenty of exercise, otherwise inactivity and boredom will lead to bad habits.

Exercise is more than just great fun for your dog. It is also vital for its physical and emotional well-being. It improves blood circulation and will enhance your dog's heart and lung function, giving it energy and stamina. Walking is the best all-round form of exercise, especially for an older dog. If you have an energetic, healthy dog, try jogging, swimming, or just playing games. Exercise your dog in some way every day.

Games as exercise
Most dogs love playing vigorous games, such as catching a flying disk.

The well-exercised dog is less likely to get bored and to develop troublesome traits, such as persistent barking, and destructive digging and chewing. Exercise causes the release of endorphins in the brain. These chemicals give your dog a great feeling of well-being. Exercise also represents an outing with your dog's family pack, plus an affirmation of its bond with you, the pack leader. Walks, jogs, and romps give your dog mental stimulation and social interaction.

Inside job
Many toy dogs, such as this Pomeranian, may be able to get much of their exercise running around an apartment.

Old friends
Dogs of all ages need regular exercise. It helps keep their body and brain in condition.

94 Some fitness fundamentals

You want to create an exercise program for your dog that is safe. Start off slowly, be consistent and patient, and you can gradually increase the level of activity when your dog shows it is ready for more. Do not start a pup on fitness training until it is 14 months old, and increase the fitness program over several months. If your dog is old, unfit, or unhealthy, start with a daily 15-minute walk and slowly increase the duration. Swimming is great for dogs with joint problems.

Is it time yet?
Active dogs thrive on regular exercise. For this dalmatian, a walk is always on the agenda.

Limbering up

This fox terrier is being given a few gentle limb bends and stretches by its owner before embarking on an exercise routine. A warm-up may prevent your dog from pulling muscles and tendons, or from putting too much strain on its body.

Up and over

Agility trials are a fun way to give your dog an exercise session with plenty of variety. Agility trials involve directing your dog through a series of jumps and obstacles.

Favorite exercise activities

• Retrieving games
• Aerial aerobics
• Hide-and-seek
• Swimming

150 mm

200 mm

250 mm

A daily walk will provide your dog with good exercise and keep it alert, but dogs also enjoy playing games and taking part in organized activities. If full-speed dashes are your dog's delight, create a chasing toy, or throw a ball or flying disk to give your dog a good workout. If you and your dog are bored by the same old walk, agility trials, lure coursing, and herding trials may provide exercise with a difference.

Playing catch and fetch
Games involving catching or retrieving a ball or stick are favorites with most breeds.

Beware of heatstroke
The coat of these Norwegian elkhounds insulates them from heat, but other dogs with thick coats are not so lucky.

During most activities, your dog will run faster and cover more ground than you do. It may even keep going past the point of exhaustion, because it expects you to call it a day. Use your common sense, practice moderation, and watch for signs of fatigue or breathing difficulties. Avoid exercising your dog in the extreme summer heat and winter cold.

Exercise time
The best time to take your dog out for a walk is in the early morning or at dusk.

FEEDING YOUR DOG

DOGS NEED A SUPPLY OF CERTAIN
NUTRIENTS TO AID GROWTH AND HEALING,
AND TO KEEP THE IMMUNE SYSTEM IN GOOD
WORKING ORDER. GOOD NUTRITION IS
REFLECTED IN HEALTH AND VITALITY.

102 | A dog's nutritional needs

How much to feed
Most adult dogs sustain their energy levels with one meal a day.

The six basic nutrients that all animals need are clean water, proteins, carbohydrates, minerals, vitamins, and fats. A dog's individual nutritional requirements will vary, depending on factors such as whether it is active or sedentary, young or old, a working dog, suffering from a chronic or temporary health condition, pregnant, or nursing a litter of puppies.

Off to a good start
Puppies need proportionally more protein than adult dogs, to fuel their rapid growth during the first few months.

A wide range of dog food is commercially available to suit your dog's palate, and your convenience and budget. These foods come in three basic types (canned, semi-moist, and dry), and three quality levels (premium, popular, and generic). If your dog has special needs, you may need to feed it a mixture of types. You can also prepare a homemade diet, which may be good for a dog with medical problems, but it can be more expensive and time-consuming.

Commercial dog foods
1 Dogs love the taste of canned dog food.
2 Dry food is also good for your dog's teeth
3 Semi-moist food does not spoil as quickly as canned.

Adult food
When a puppy has reached 75 to 80 percent of its adult size, it is a good time to switch it to an adult diet.

Good dog
Food used as a reward for good behavior sends a clear message of approval and gives positive reinforcement.

Treats are a great way to reward your dog for learning commands and tricks—or for just being your best friend. But many snacks and treats tend to be high in calories and not nutritionally balanced. Like all good things, they should be given in moderation, especially if your dog is overweight or has another health problem.

Common snacks and treats
- Chewy treats
- Biscuits
- Fruits and vegetables
- Bones
- Dog cookies

There are all kinds of dog snacks and treats; even low-calorie treats for dogs that need to shed a few pounds. If your dog follows a specific diet for medical reasons, ask your vet to recommend an appropriate treat. Avoid chocolate, which contains a stimulant that can make dogs seriously ill.

Fresh and dry
Fruits and vegetables (above) will reward your dog while helping to keep its teeth clean and its breath fresh. The selection of dry snacks (below) includes jerky (top), puppy biscuits (left), and dog cookies (right), which are all tasty treats for your dog.

Feeding equipment

Automatic feeder
A timer makes the lid of the feeder open automatically.

Well-designed food and water bowls will make your dog's meals more enjoyable and less messy for you. Dog bowls can be metal, plastic, or ceramic, and your dog will need one for food and one for water. A good bowl is sturdy, easy to clean, will not tip over easily, and has plenty of room for your dog's muzzle. Some special bowls have moats around them that will keep out ants and other crawling insects.

Is it time yet?
Dogs are creatures of habit
and they like to eat at the
same time every day, but it is
not always possible to be there
when your dog is expecting
its evening meal. An automatic
feeding and watering system
(far left) may be the answer
to this dog's plea.

110 | The right weight

What is ideal?

1 Underweight: Ribs easy to feel; raised, bony tail structure; an abdominal tuck with a marked hourglass shape.

2 Ideal weight: Ribs possible to feel; smooth tail structure; an abdominal tuck with a well-proportioned "waist."

3 Obese: Ribs difficult to feel; thickened tail structure; pendulous, bulging belly; no "waist;" very broad back.

The amount of food a dog requires varies with the individual dog. Do not overnourish your dog. Giving food formulated for an active young dog to a sedentary old one will not make it any healthier—just fatter. Instead, evaluate your dog's needs and adjust its rations accordingly.

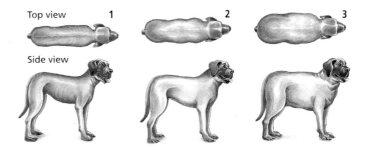

Top view 1 2 3

Side view

Too much of a good thing
Overweight dogs, such as this corgi, are at a much higher risk for many different health conditions. Effective weight control is essential.

Water is as important to your dog as oxygen. It is necessary to maintain proper levels of body fluids so that nutrients can be carried throughout the body and wastes can be eliminated. Dogs can go for a while without food, but without water they become dehydrated, or suffer heatstroke, and perish within a few days. An adult dog's body is 60 to 70 percent water; a puppy's is more than 80 percent. You need never be concerned about giving a dog "too much" water. However, if you notice a marked increase in its water consumption, you should talk to your vet.

Good medicine
By regularly drinking water, this Labrador mix is helping its kidneys work better.

Cool and fresh
Most dogs love to drink from the hose. Just make sure the water running through is cool before you allow it to drink.

GROOMING

GROOMING IS NOT JUST A MATTER OF
LOOKING GOOD; IT IS VITAL FOR YOUR
DOG'S HEALTH AND HYGIENE. MAKE
GROOMING SESSIONS PART OF YOUR DOG'S
PREVENTIVE HEALTH PROGRAM.

116 | Different dog coats

Long, double coat
Chow chows have a long, straight, coarse outer coat, with a very thick undercoat.

To know how best to groom your dog, you need to determine the type of coat it has. All dogs' coats fall into one of these eight categories.

Hairless coat
Chinese cresteds have little or no body hair.

Short, double coat
Labradors have a soft, thin undercoat.

Short, smooth coat
Basenjis have a short coat, with no undercoat

Short, wiry coat
Irish terriers have a hard double coat of hair that is thick and wiry.

Long, coarse coat
Tibetan terriers have a coarse coat, with a softer undercoat.

Curly coat
The thick, curly coat of poodles does not shed.

Long, silky coat
Maltese terriers have no undercoat.

Grooming tools

Tools of the trade
Buy the appropriate grooming equipment for your dog's coat type. Ask the breeder for tips.

Regular grooming keeps your dog clean and looking its best. It also keeps shedding to a minimum and gives you the chance to inspect your dog to make sure its skin, teeth, eyes, ears, and nails are healthy. The right grooming equipment is essential, and there is a wide range of brushes and combs to choose from. A combined approach—brushing your dog, and following with a thorough combing—will remove huge amounts of excess hair.

Wide-toothed comb

Mat splitter

Hound glove

Double-sided grooming glove

Combined bristle and pin brush

Pincushion brush

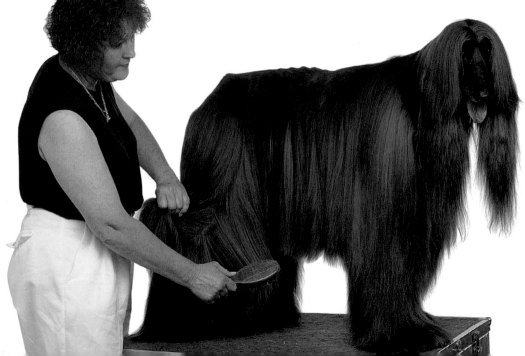

There is a basic technique for grooming each of the coat types found in dogs. Because grooming is so important, it is vital that you teach your dog to tolerate it. Bristle brushes are best used on dogs with short coats, while pin brushes suit long-coated breeds. Large-toothed combs are used to remove the undercoat in heavy-coated dogs. Mat splitters saw through mats in your dog's coat and a hound glove gives your dog's coat a polished look.

An elegant coat
A pin brush is being used to keep this Afghan hound's coat looking beautiful.

Medium-length coat
A border collie's longish double coat needs a pin brush or a wide-toothed comb.

A close shave

This Bedlington terrier (below) requires specialized clipping every six weeks. If you want to do this at home, make sure you invest in good-quality blades and clipping equipment (below right).

Many breeds of dog can benefit from some tidying up with clippers, whether at home or in the salon. Although mastery of the art of clipping belongs to the professional groomer, you too can use these instruments to groom your dog and make it look good. You will need to practice a lot—it takes quite a bit of skill to clip a dog's coat properly. It is best to keep your dog in a simple clip that is easy to maintain. Always cut with the hair, not against it. You will need to use two types of clippers—standard for all-around grooming, and small for the face, ears, and feet.

The "lion" clip
This standard poodle has been given the sculpted "lion" clip, which usually is given only to show dogs.

Breeds that need clipping
- Poodles
- Bichon frises
- Bedlington terriers
- Schnauzers
- Airedale terriers

124 | Ears and eyes

Cleaning eyes
Use a moistened cotton ball or piece of gauze and wipe from the center toward the outside.

Grooming your dog's ears can keep them looking and smelling good; wiping its eyes will keep them sparkling and clear. Regular grooming also gives you an opportunity to check its eyes and ears for any signs of problems in their earliest stages. Start cleaning your dog's eyes and ears when it is a puppy. The ears should be cleaned once a month. Use a cotton ball moistened with mineral oil or an ear-cleaning solution. Some dogs have hairy ears, which means that there is more chance of dampness and possible infection. If your dog has hair that falls into its eyes, you should cut it, or tie it back. If you notice any redness, cloudiness, swelling, or excess weepiness of the eyes, take your dog to the vet.

Problem ears

Dogs with long, floppy ears, such as this bloodhound, are especially prone to ear problems because the design of their ears prevents air from circulating. Ears like these need special attention.

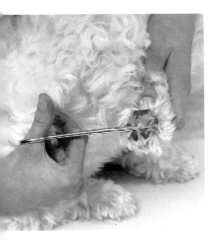

Trimming paw hair
Regular trimming keeps the
feet drier and healthier.

Basic paw care is a vital part of your dog's health care
routine. Your dog's feet probably take more of a pounding
than any other part of its body. To protect its pads from
damage, rub vitamin E and juice from an aloe plant onto
them before and after exercise. Dogs that regularly walk on
concrete wear down their nails and rarely need to have them
trimmed. Other dogs will need to have them trimmed every
four weeks. Be conservative in your cutting. Take off only
the thin, curved nail tip. Since the hair on your dog's feet
traps moisture and dirt, you should trim it with scissors.

Neat nails

Hold your dog's paw firmly. Sharp trimmers will prevent the nails from splitting.

Trimming tips

- Avoid cutting the quick
- Cut at downward curve
- Smooth with a nail file
- Trim hair between toes

128 Clean teeth

Dental hygiene
Brushing your dog's teeth
is not difficult if you use
a specially designed dog
toothbrush (top) or "finger"
toothbrush (bottom).

An important, but often overlooked, part of your dog's daily grooming routine is the brushing of its teeth. If you do not brush your dog's teeth regularly, plaque builds up on the teeth and under the gums. If this is not removed, a bacterial infection can develop, which can enter the bloodstream and potentially spread to your dog's liver, heart, or brain. You should brush your dog's teeth at least twice a week and have them examined by a vet once a year. Do not use human toothpastes that contain detergents and other chemicals. Dogs cannot rinse and spit, so their toothpaste must be edible.

Open wide!
If your dog is small, like this dachshund, pay close attention to its dental hygiene. A smaller mouth is more prone to tooth loss and gum disease.

When it is time for a bath

Dogs do not need baths all that often, but even the most fastidious dogs need regular baths and, depending on their coats, some dogs need them more often than others. A dog that spends a lot of time outside tends to get dirtier than an indoor dog, but most dogs are bathed at least two or three times a year. Bathing is the best way to remove the grease and dander that cause a mousy smell. You can choose an all-purpose shampoo or one that is more specialized, such as an oatmeal, hypoallergenic, or medicated shampoo.

Soaping up
Many kinds of dog shampoos are commercially available from pet supply stores.

Outdoor bathing
If the weather is warm, bathing your dog outside will minimize mess.

| Bathing techniques

Professional finish
Blow-drying a long coat prevents mats. It stops your dog from getting cold, too.

Bathtime will go much more smoothly if you are well prepared. Before you bathe your dog, you should brush it to remove the dead hair and loosen the dirt, making it easier to wash away. Always use lukewarm, not hot, water. Use a shampoo that is specially formulated for dogs and be sure to rinse thoroughly. Some dogs can be left to dry naturally, others need the help of a portable hair dryer.

Do not forget feet
If water and shampoo are left to dry between the toes, the feet will get itchy. Rinse thoroughly, then get your fingers between the toes to dry them properly.

HEALTH CARE

MAKING SURE THAT YOUR DOG LIVES A
LONG AND HEALTHY LIFE MEANS PROVIDING
NOT ONLY A WELL-BALANCED DIET AND
PLENTY OF EXERCISE, BUT ALSO GOOD
PREVENTIVE HEALTH CARE.

Vaccines will prevent your dog from contracting many of the common diseases, such as rabies, parvovirus, distemper, heartworm, and Lyme disease. These annual vaccinations are a vital investment in your dog's good health. Visit your vet as soon as possible after obtaining your pup. At your first visit, the vet will do a physical examination, administer worming medication, and set up a vaccination schedule. Your pup should also have dental check-ups at regular intervals.

Choosing a vet
Find a vet to suit you. Ask your dog-owning friends to recommend a vet, or call a humane society for a referral.

A treat for the heart
Heartworm prevention tablets can be fed to your dog like chewy treats. There is also a vaccine available (bottom opposite) that is given annually.

Less stress
This Old English sheepdog–
border collie mix is more
relaxed if treated by its owner.

Points to check
- Breathing
- Heart rate
- Fluid levels
- Circulation
- Temperature

The best way to keep your dog healthy is to notice the first signs of a problem before it becomes serious. The best way to do this is to give it a complete once-over every week. Check your dog's breathing—at rest it should be slow, steady, and quiet, about 20 to 30 breaths a minute. Also check your dog's heart rate—it should be between 60 and 150 beats per minute, depending on its size. Your dog's temperature should be between 99.5° and 102°F (37.5°–39°C). Anything over 104°F (40°C) rates medical attention. Never hesitate to seek your vet's help if you need it.

Checking heart rate
Take your dog's pulse by placing your fingers on the femoral artery in the inside of the thigh. Ask your vet what the normal rate is for your dog.

When checking over your dog, start by looking at its ears, then move on to its eyes, nose, mouth, body, legs, tail, and paws. Always consult your vet if something does not appear right to you, or if you notice such signs as: loss of appetite for more than a day; difficulty eating; sudden weight loss or gain; fever; vomiting; or change in bowel habits for more than a day.

Healthy and happy
This energetic and bright-eyed wirehaired fox terrier is the picture of doggy good health.

Eyes
Clear and bright; pupils equal size; membranes a healthy pink.

Skin
Smooth; clean; dry; pliable; odorless; parasite-free.

Nose
Cool and wet; free of discharge.

Tongue and teeth
Tongue: Bright pink; moist.
Teeth. White; no buildup of tartar.

Ribs
Not too prominent; not covered with thick padding of fat.

Feet, pads, and nails
Feet: No mats, sores, or debris.
Pads: No cuts or blisters.
Nails: Trimmed.

Body and coat
Body: Pain-free; no rigidity.
Coat: Clean, shiny, unmatted; no bald spots.

142 Giving medicines

Giving pills

1 Hold pill between forefinger and thumb and push jaw down with other fingers. Place pill in center of tongue, as far back as possible.

2 Hold the dog's mouth shut until it licks its nose, showing it has swallowed. Help by massaging its throat.

From time to time, your dog may need some medication to treat a health problem. Although some drugs are administered by your vet, most will be given by you at home. Always give medications gently and properly—not only to ensure that your dog gets better, but to prevent it from getting "head shy." If possible, you should enlist a friend's help to hold your dog still and calm it.

1

2

Giving liquid medicines

Use a dropper or needleless syringe to draw up the correct dose. Insert the end of the dropper or syringe into your dog's mouth and gently squeeze in the liquid. Give your dog time to swallow.

Common medicines

• Pills
• Liquid medicines
• Eye drops
• Ear drops

Items to keep at hand

- List of emergency contacts
- First-aid manual
- First-aid kit

For minor injuries and ailments, treating your dog at home is not only less expensive and more convenient, it is less stressful for you and your dog. And if your dog is ever seriously ill or injured, first aid is vital to stabilize it before rushing it to a vet. Make sure you keep an up-to-date first-aid kit handy. Scrapes and cuts can easily be treated at home. Clean the wound using sterile pads and warm, soapy water. Rinse, dry, and apply antibiotic cream twice a day until it heals. Bandage if necessary, and if in doubt, see your vet.

First-aid kit

A first-aid kit for your dog can be the difference between life and death. Your kit should include such items as tweezers, ice pack, and bandages (left).

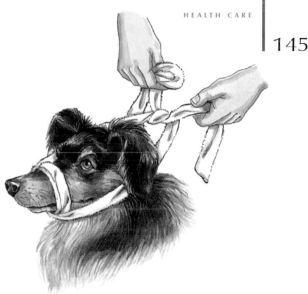

An improvised muzzle

1 Tie a loose knot in a strip of material to create a large loop. Slip the loop over your dog's nose to about halfway up and draw it tight.

2 Bring the ends downward and cross them over each other under the dog's chin. Carry the ends behind the back of its ears and tie a knot.

Moving a dog

1 For a large dog, slide a blanket under it. Wrap the dog in the blanket and move as one unit.

2 For a small dog, carefully lift it with both hands to support its whole body. Try to let any fractured limbs dangle.

Knowing how to recognize and react to common emergencies may save your dog's life. Your goal should be to prevent further injury, and minimize pain and distress, while seeking veterinary care. Learn how to deal with the most common emergencies, such as car accidents, heatstroke, bleeding, and poisoning.

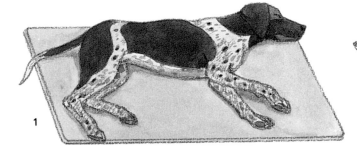

1

2

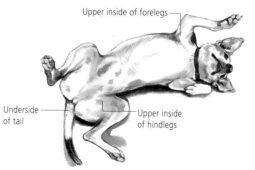

Broken leg
Splint leg with firm material,
bind in place with cloth strips,
and take the dog to the vet.

Pressure points
To reduce bleeding, apply firm
pressure to whichever one of
these points is between the
wound and the heart.

Upper inside of forelegs

Underside
of tail

Upper inside
of hindlegs

A near-drowned dog

Clear any discharge from its nose and mouth. Hold dog by its hindlegs and swing it gently back and forth to drain the water from its lungs.

In the event of an accident, immediate action may be required. Quickly recognizing, then solving, the problem is critically important to your dog. If your dog is not breathing and/or has no heartbeat, you should administer cardiopulmonary resuscitation (CPR) and call your vet as soon as possible.

Cardiac massage

Lie your dog on its side. Place the heel of your right hand on the ribs over its heart. Place your left hand over your right and push down so that you press the chest halfway to the ground. Compress 15 times, then breathe into its nose twice. Repeat the process, compressing the heart 80 to 100 times per minute.

Mouth-to-nose resuscitation
1 Lay dog on side and open its airway. Remove foreign bodies from mouth. Extend head back and pull tongue forward. Check that nostrils are clear.
2 Hold dog's mouth closed. Place your mouth over nostrils and blow four times, hard enough to make its chest rise.
2 Pause to allow air to exit lungs, then repeat. Keep blowing until the dog resumes normal breathing.

HEALTH PROBLEMS

YOU CANNOT EXPECT YOUR DOG TO BE
PERFECTLY HEALTHY ALL THE TIME. LEARN TO
RECOGNIZE THE EARLY SIGNS OF ILLNESS AND
ALWAYS ASK YOUR VETERINARIAN FOR HELP.
REMEMBER, YOUR DOG DEPENDS ON YOU.

152 | Aging

Apart from the giant breeds, a dog that is well cared for can be expected to live for about 12 years. But as dogs age, they become more susceptible to a number of health problems. The effects can be minimized by taking a little extra care and being sensitive to your dog's changing needs. While some problems are an inevitable part of aging, others are actually illnesses that can be successfully treated. Contact your vet to discuss any symptoms you notice. In the meantime, adjust your dog's diet as its metabolism slows down, and keep its joints supple with gentle daily walks.

Eye disease
Cataracts are a common problem in older dogs.

Elder statesman
Your dog may experience problems similar to those caused by senility in people. It may forget its training, or its responses may be slower. New drugs and retraining can improve its quality of life.

Common problems of aging
- Arthritis
- Kidney failure
- Dental disease
- Diabetes
- Eye disease

154 | Coughing and sneezing

Breathing problems
Dogs with pushed-in faces,
such as pugs, are prone to
respiratory problems.

To ease symptoms
• Moisten the air with
  a humidifier
• Give your dog a cough
  suppressant
• Give your dog plenty
  of fluids

All dogs cough and sneeze occasionally, but when the odd "eck" becomes hacking, you can assume your dog has a serious respiratory disorder. Conditions such as kennel cough rarely last long, but other coughs may be more serious. If the problem is frequent or persists for more than two days, you should visit your vet.

Ease off on exercise

While your dog has a cough, go easy on the exercise. Use a harness rather than a collar or choke chain, which may be uncomfortable and irritate its sore throat.

Common causes of coughing and sneezing

- Kennel cough
- Old age
- Genetic conditions
- Heart failure
- Heartworm
- Allergies

156 | Ears

Giving eardrops
1 Hold the ear flap firmly and squeeze out required number of drops. Let them run down the underside of the ear flap.
2 Still holding the flap, gently massage the base of the ear to work the drops right in.

Your dog's ears contain its balance-control center, so even minor problems can be very uncomfortable. Without treatment, ear infections can lead to deafness or the need for major surgery. You should suspect problems if your dog is frequently scratching or shaking its head, or if its ears seem unusually tender. If it has a head tilt, or seems dizzy or deaf, seek help immediately to prevent permanent damage.

1

2

Suspect a problem?
Use a flashlight to
check for foreign
objects in ears.

Common ear problems
• Infections
• Ear mites
• Hematomas
• Ear flap injuries

Warm compress

A wad of gauze soaked in a warm saline solution may help reduce the pain of a sore eye.

Common eye problems

- Conjunctivitis
- "Dry eye"
- Cataracts
- Retinal disease
- Corneal injuries
- Eyelid abnormalities

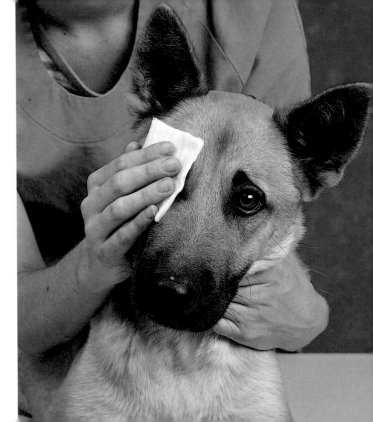

Common eye conditions produce discharge, redness, and pain—usually signaled by tearing, squinting, and holding the eye closed. The eyes will usually recover as long as the problem is treated quickly; however, some problems are genetic, and may need surgery. Cloudiness in the eyes often happens to a dog as it gets older. If you notice that your dog negotiates obstacles poorly or stumbles on steps, take it to the vet to make sure it is nothing serious.

Applying eye ointment
1 Holding the eye open, squeeze a little of the ointment into the corner of the eye nearest the nose.
2 To spread the ointment over the eye, first allow the dog to close it, then gently massage the eyelids together.

1

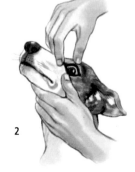

2

160 | Gastrointestinal problems

Lock temptation away
Diarrhea may be because of infection, or a dog eating something it should not, like yesterday's trash.

Common gastrointestinal problems
• Diarrhea
• Vomiting
• Bloat
• Flatulence
• Constipation

All dogs vomit and get diarrhea during their lives, and some breeds are more gassy than others. These problems are mostly minor and have commonsense solutions. Maintaining a steady diet, introducing new foods gradually, and keeping water sources clean, trash cans tightly closed, and food refrigerated, will help prevent upsets. But some gastrointestinal problems are more serious and require professional attention. If your dog has persistent diarrhea or vomiting, or has blood in its stools or vomit, seek the advice of your vet.

Flea patrol

Regular combing with a fine-toothed comb, such as those below, will keep your dog's coat flea free. Dip the comb into hot water or rubbing alcohol after each stroke to kill fleas that are picked up.

Fighting fleas and worms |

Small, flat, hopping insects called fleas are by far the most common skin parasites that plague dogs. Their bites lead to itching, chewing, and scratching, most notably at the base of the tail. Check for fleas whenever your dog shows persistent scratching. Pay attention to problem areas, such as behind your dog's ears, on its rump, or between its hindlegs. Intestinal worms are very common—most puppies are born with them. Dogs may also get tapeworms from ingesting fleas. Happily, there are now more treatments on hand to combat infestations of both kinds of parasite.

Common worms

Adult worms can sometimes be seen in your dog's feces, but the vet may need to do a microscopic examination of the feces to determine which kind of worm it has. Below are the most common varieties of worm.

Roundworms

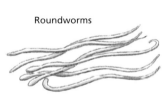

Tapeworm

Whipworms

164 | Mouth and teeth

Prevent dental problems
The best way to prevent plaque buildup is to keep your dog's teeth, gums, and mouth in as good a condition as this Siberian husky's.

While dogs do not usually get cavities, more than 85 percent suffer from periodontal disease by the age of four. This causes damage around the teeth and can develop into gingivitis, which damages the gums. The main cause is the buildup of plaque, a thin, sticky, bacteria-laden substance that forms on the teeth. Regular brushing will help remove plaque. And, because tartar develops from plaque, if you stop the plaque from settling, the tartar does not stand a chance. Hard, crunchy snacks and kibble, or compressed biscuits coated with anti-plaque and anti-tartar ingredients, are great, too. However, annual check-ups are the best way to ensure that any problems are caught early.

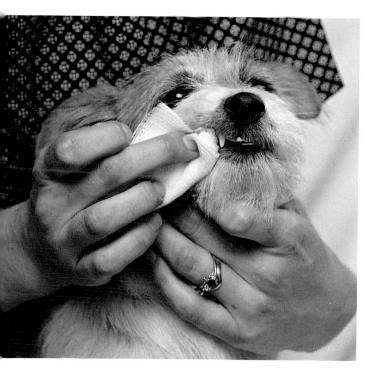

Regular, routine care

Clean your dog's teeth at least twice a week and choose a hard chew toy (below) to help dislodge particles from under your dog's gum margins.

Common mouth problems

- Dental disease
- Broken teeth
- Drooling
- Mouth infections

166 | Orthopedics

Prone to problems

The dachshund's long spine has made the dog vulnerable to disk disease. Mild slippage of the spinal disks may cause discomfort only, but severe slippage can cause paralysis. Severe disk disease requires immediate surgery.

Common orthopedic problems

- Arthritis
- Dysplasia
- Back pain

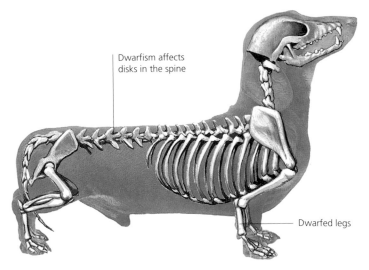

Dwarfism affects disks in the spine

Dwarfed legs

Veterinary surveys suggest that 20 percent of adult dogs will develop osteoarthritis. Also known as degenerative joint disease, it is the most common type of arthritis and may affect any joint. However, genetic defects such as hip dysplasia trouble many breeds at an early age and require a lifetime of care. For routine osteoarthritis and for back pain, a combination of anti-inflammatory medication and weight reduction is usually recommended. Treatment of dysplasia may involve surgery.

Loose and limber
A soft bed will ease the aches of your aging dog. On cold, wet days, a warm blanket or hot water bottle offers extra comfort. Also, try a gentle massage of the sore areas to ease their stiffness.

168 | Skin conditions

Problem licking
Sometimes dogs will lick at the same spot until they create a large, open wound—a condition called acral lick dermatitis or lick granuloma.

Skin conditions are probably the most common canine medical problems that vets treat. The signs of skin disease include itchiness, dandruff, hair loss, crusting, redness, odors, or lumps. Severe scratching, rubbing, and licking can lead to skin infections. If your dog is scratching and there are no signs of parasites, take it to the vet. It may have an allergy, a fungal infection such as ringworm, or it may be harboring mites, which can cause mange. Dandruff is common, but if the flaking is accompanied by a dull, greasy coat and a bad odor, it may be a disorder called seborrhea. Your vet can provide treatment.

Sun protection

A dog with little pigment or a short white coat should have sunscreen on its ear tips, belly, and nose. Avoid creams with zinc or PABA, which can be dangerous if licked.

Common skin problems

- Allergies
- Hot spots (acral lick dermatitis)
- Ringworm
- Mange
- Dandruff

Urinary tract problems

There are many causes of urinary tract problems, ranging from infections to prostate disease, and they may signal other, serious, conditions. Bladder control problems are never normal, and a dog that urinates frequently, or without control, may be suffering from diabetes or liver disease. Increased urination and thirst may also mean kidney failure or diabetes, while recurrent cystitis and bloody urine can signal kidney stones. Seek veterinary advice immediately.

Doggie diapers
For dogs with bladder control problems, these products will keep both fur and carpets dry.

Endless supply
Urinary tract infections can give dogs an urgent, frequent need to urinate what may be only small amounts.

172 | Weight problems

Portly pooches
Some breeds are susceptible to obesity, including Labrador retrievers (below), bulldogs, basset hounds, and beagles.

Obesity is the number one nutrition-related disease in dogs. Sometimes a metabolic disease, such as hypothyroidism, triggers obesity. Some breeds put on weight easily and require special attention to their feeding needs. However, most overweight dogs simply eat too much and exercise too little. Being overweight can lead to diminished quality as well as quantity of life for your dog, so do a rib test. If you cannot find its ribs, it is diet and exercise time. Rapid weight loss, however, can be a sign of something serious. If you notice any sudden changes, seek help immediately.

The rib test
At a healthy weight, your dog will have a distinct waist and you will be able to feel just a slight amount of padding over the ribs.

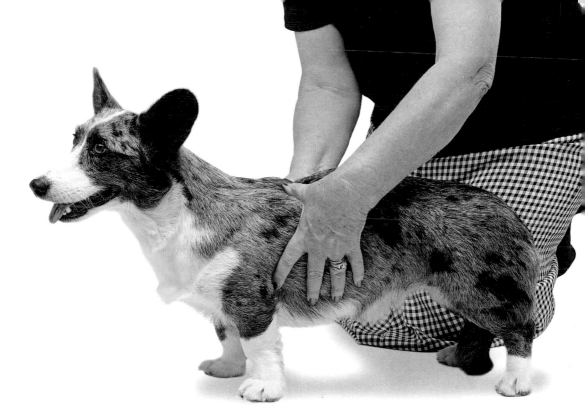

Dog breeds

176 How to use the guide

If you are interested in becoming the proud owner of a purebred dog, this is the place to start. This guide provides details of more than 60 of the most popular dog breeds.

Brave, curious, lively ——————— **Temperament**
Summary of temperament

Regular brushing ——————— **Grooming**
Preferred type of grooming

Regular, moderate ——————— **Exercise**
Type and frequency

Ideal for apartment living —— **Living conditions**
Preferred environment

Good watchdog ——————— **Watchdog**
Summary of ability

♂ Standard: male ——————— **Size and weight male**
About 8 in (20 cm)   Average size for males
20–22 lb (9–10 kg)

♀ Standard: female ——————— **Size and weight female**
About 8 in (20 cm)   Average size for females
18–20 lb (8–9 kg)

Name of breed
As used by the American Kennel Club

Label
Specific to dog pictured

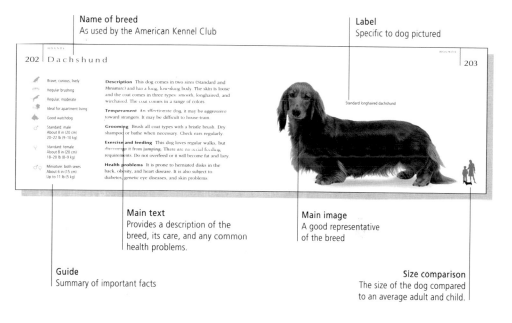

202 | Dachshund

Brave, curious, lively

Regular brushing

Regular: moderate

Ideal for apartment living

Good watchdog

Standard: male
About 8 in (20 cm)
20–22 lb (9–10 kg)

Standard: female
About 8 in (20 cm)
18–20 lb (8–9 kg)

Miniature: both sexes
About 6 in (15 cm)
Up to 11 lb (5 kg)

Description This dog comes in two sizes (Standard and Miniature) and has a long, low-slung body. The skin is loose and the coat comes in three types: smooth, longhaired, and wirehaired. The coat comes in a range of colors.

Temperament An affectionate dog, it may be aggressive toward strangers. It may be difficult to house-train.

Grooming Brush all coat types with a bristle brush. Dry shampoo or bathe when necessary. Check ears regularly.

Exercise and feeding This dog loves regular walks, but discourage it from jumping. There are no special feeding requirements. Do not overfeed or it will become fat and lazy.

Health problems It is prone to herniated disks in the back, obesity, and heart disease. It is also subject to diabetes, genetic eye diseases, and skin problems.

Standard longhaired dachshund

Main text
Provides a description of the breed, its care, and any common health problems.

Main image
A good representative of the breed

Guide
Summary of important facts

Size comparison
The size of the dog compared to an average adult and child.

SPORTING DOGS

THESE DOGS ARE INTELLIGENT, RESPONSIVE
AND TRUSTWORTHY. ALTHOUGH MANY
SPORTING DOGS BECOME NOISY AND
DESTRUCTIVE IF CONFINED, THEY ARE EASY
TO TRAIN AND PATIENT WITH CHILDREN.

Brittany

Rugged, friendly, energetic

Regular brushing

Regular, vigorous

Adapts well to urban living, but needs plenty of exercise

Good watchdog

♂ Male
18–21 in (46–53 cm)
30–45 lb (14–20 kg)

♀ Female
18–20 in (46–51 cm)
30–40 lb (14–18 kg)

Description Graceful and well-muscled, this dog has a dense coat that comes in white with orange, black, brown, or liver, as well as tricolors and roans. The short tail is usually docked a little.

Temperament Easy to train and handle, the Brittany is a loving and gentle dog, always eager to please.

Grooming Twice-weekly brushing of the flat coat is needed. Bathe or dry shampoo a few times a year.

Exercise and feeding This dog has plenty of stamina and needs vigorous activity to stay in peak condition. There are no special feeding requirements.

Health problems Generally a hardy breed, the Brittany is prone to ear infections, spinal paralysis, and eye diseases, such as glaucoma.

English cocker spaniel

Joyful, affectionate, intelligent

Regular brushing

Regular, moderate to vigorous

Adapts well to urban living, but needs plenty of exercise

Good watchdog

Male
15–17 in (38–43 cm)
28–32 lb (13–15 kg)

Female
14–16 in (36–41 cm)
26–30 lb (12–14 kg)

Description A strong dog with a sturdy body, it has a silky coat that comes in solid reds, black, golden, and liver, as well as black and tan, particolors, tricolors, and roans.

Temperament This breed enjoys family life, but needs firm training. Some dogs are prone to behavioral disorders that may cause aggression, so check the dog's family history.

Grooming Brush and comb three times a week. Shedding can be a problem. Bathe or dry shampoo as necessary. The ears and the hair on the feet need special care.

Exercise and feeding Long daily walks and weekly runs are a must. There are no special feeding requirements.

Health problems The breed suffers from genetic eye diseases, and skin and kidney problems. It is also prone to diabetes and infections.

English springer spaniel

Playful, cheerful, loyal

Regular brushing

Regular, moderate

Adapts well to urban living, but needs plenty of exercise

Good watchdog

♂ Male
19–21 in (48–53 cm)
45–55 lb (20–25 kg)

♀ Female
18–20 in (46–51 cm)
40–50 lb (18–23 kg)

Description This is a strong, sturdy dog, with a soft, water-repellent coat that comes in all spaniel colors, but mainly white with liver or black. The tail is usually docked.

Temperament This dog enjoys company and is patient with children. However, the breed is prone to an inherited behavioral disorder that may cause aggression, so always check the dog's family history.

Grooming Extra care is needed when the dog is molting. Bathe or dry shampoo when necessary. Check ears regularly.

Exercise and feeding The springer spaniel enjoys lots of exercise. There are no special feeding requirements.

Health problems This spaniel is susceptible to ear infections, eye diseases, allergic skin conditions, and elbow and hip dysplasia.

Intelligent, reliable, keen

Regular brushing; wirehaired needs more than shorthaired

Regular, vigorous

Adapts well to urban living, but needs plenty of space and exercise

Good watchdog

Male
22–26 in (56–66 cm)
50–65 lb (23–29 kg)

Female
21–25 in (53–63 cm)
45–60 lb (20–27 kg)

Description There are two varieties: the shorthaired comes in solid black or liver; the wirehaired comes in solid liver, liver and white, roan, or black and white.

Temperament An affectionate pet, this dog can be hard to train. Both types are good with families, but may overwhelm younger children. The wirehaired may be aggressive.

Grooming The shorthaired's coat is easy to groom. The wirehaired's coat needs attention. Bathe every few months. Check ears and feet regularly.

Exercise and feeding Exercise is of utmost importance for this dog. There are no special feeding requirements.

Health problems Generally hardy and long lived, this breed is prone to ear infections, hip and elbow dysplasia, von Willebrand's disease, eye diseases, and skin cancers.

Shorthaired German pointer

188 Labrador retriever

Reliable, patient, gentle

Regular brushing

Regular, vigorous

Adapts well to urban living, but needs plenty of exercise

Good watchdog

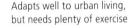

♂ Male
22–24 in (56–61 cm)
50–60 lb (23–27 kg)

♀ Female
21–23 in (53–58 cm)
45–55 lb (20–25 kg)

Description This strong, solid dog has a sturdy frame, a broad skull, and a powerful neck. The coat comes in solid black, yellow, gold, fawn, cream, or chocolate. The tail is thick at the base, and round and tapered along its length.

Temperament Exceptionally patient and gentle with children, this dog is obedient and easy to train. Never aggressive toward people, some may fight other dogs.

Grooming Comb and brush twice a week. Bathe or dry shampoo only when necessary.

Exercise and feeding This dog loves exercise, especially swimming. There are no special feeding requirements.

Health problems It is prone to hip and elbow dysplasia. It may also suffer from epilepsy, diabetes, and hereditary eye diseases, such as cataracts and progressive retinal atrophy.

190 | Golden retriever

Calm, affectionate, gentle

Daily combing and brushing

Regular, vigorous

Adapts well to urban living, but needs plenty of space

Good watchdog

Male
22–24 in (56–61 cm)
60–80 lb (27–36 kg)

Female
20–22 in (51–56 cm)
55–70 lb (25–32 kg)

Description This graceful and elegant dog has a lustrous coat in any shade of gold or cream. The hair lies flat or in gentle waves around its neck, shoulders, and hips.

Temperament The intelligent golden retriever is easy to train and is almost always patient and gentle with children. An occasional few display aggressive behavior.

Grooming The coat sheds heavily, but daily grooming will help. Use a firm bristle brush, paying particular attention to the dense undercoat. Dry shampoo regularly.

Exercise and feeding This breed loves long, daily walks and any other forms of exercise, especially swimming. There are no special feeding requirements.

Health problems It is prone to skin, eye, heart, and orthopedic conditions, as well as von Willebrand's disease.

192 Chesapeake Bay retriever

Keen worker, can
be aggressive

Regular brushing

Regular, vigorous; loves
to swim

Adapts to urban living, but
best with access to country

Good watchdog

Male
23–26 in (58–66 cm)
65–80 lb (29–36 kg)

Female
21–24 in (53–61 cm)
55–70 lb (25–32 kg)

Description A strong, athletic dog, this breed has a tight, dense, wavy, totally water-resistant coat, and webbed feet. The coat color varies from dark tan to dark brown. It is a strong swimmer and can swim even in heavy seas.

Temperament Courageous and intelligent, this breed can be tricky to train. It may be aggressive with other dogs.

Grooming Brush the dense, harsh, shorthaired coat regularly. Bathe only if necessary.

Exercise and feeding This dog needs a great deal of vigorous activity, including swimming, to stay in peak condition. There are no special feeding requirements.

Health problems While this breed is generally very healthy, some dogs may suffer from hip dysplasia and hereditary eye diseases.

Weimaraner

Intelligent, friendly, powerful

Regular brushing

Regular, vigorous

Adapts well to urban living, but needs plenty of exercise

Excellent watchdog

Male
24–27 in (61–69 cm)
55–70 lb (25–32 kg)

Female
22–25 in (56–63 cm)
50–65 lb (23–29 kg)

Description This athletic dog has a sleek, close-fitting coat that comes in silver-gray to mouse shades. The eyes are blue-gray or amber. The tail is usually docked.

Temperament This strong-willed dog needs firm, thorough training to control its tendency to dominate and be aggressive. It is good with children.

Grooming The coat does not shed much and needs brushing only once a week. Dry shampoo occasionally and bathe with mild soap only when necessary.

Exercise and feeding This dog thrives on regular exercise. Feed it two or three small meals a day to avoid bloat.

Health problems A generally hardy breed, it is prone to bloat, and can suffer from hip dysplasia and various skin ailments. It is also prone to sunburn on the nose.

HOUNDS

HOUNDS WERE BRED TO HUNT GAME.
SOME WERE BRED FOR THEIR SPEED, AND
SOME FOR THEIR EXTRAORDINARY SENSES OF
SMELL AND SIGHT. THESE DAYS MOST ARE
KEPT AS INTELLIGENT, LIVELY, AND LOYAL PETS.

Basset hound

Gentle and loyal

Weekly brushing, paying attention to ears and feet

Regular, moderate

Well suited to urban living

Not a good watchdog

♂ Male
12–15 in (30–38 cm)
50–65 lb (23–29 kg)

♀ Female
11–14 in (28–36 cm)
45–60 lb (20–27 kg)

Description This dog has short, stocky legs on which the skin is loose and folded. The body is sturdy and barrel-shaped. The coat comes in combinations of white with tan, black, and lemon. The long ears are velvety.

Temperament The basset is a good-natured dog, sociable and gentle with children. However, it can be stubborn, and is one of the most difficult breeds to house-train.

Grooming Brush with a firm bristle brush and shampoo only when necessary. Wipe the ears every week.

Exercise and feeding Short daily walks are important, but keep it from jumping and stressing the forelegs. Feed two or three small meals a day to avoid bloat. Do not overfeed.

Health problems This breed suffers from bloat, spinal disk problems, glaucoma, and ear and skin infections.

200 Beagle

Alert, joyful, even-tempered

Weekly brushing to remove dead hair

Regular, moderate

Adapts well to urban living

Not a good watchdog

♂ Male
14–16 in (36–41 cm)
22–25 lb (10–11 kg)

♀ Female
13–15 in (33–38 cm)
20–23 lb (9–10 kg)

Description This muscular little dog has a dense, waterproof coat. It comes in combinations of white, black, tan, red, lemon, and blue mottle.

Temperament Rarely aggressive, this dog is strong-willed and not easy to train. If bored, it may become destructive; if lonely, it may bark a lot, or wander.

Grooming Use a firm bristle brush and dry shampoo occasionally. Check the ears and keep the nails trimmed.

Exercise and feeding The beagle needs brisk, daily exercise to stay in shape. There are no special feeding requirements, but take care that it does not become obese.

Health problems In addition to obesity, it is prone to epilepsy, genetic eye and bleeding disorders, skin and spinal problems, and heart disease.

Dachshund

Brave, curious, lively

Regular brushing

Regular, moderate

Ideal for apartment living

Good watchdog

♂ Standard: male
About 8 in (20 cm)
20–22 lb (9–10 kg)

♀ Standard: female
About 8 in (20 cm)
18–20 lb (8–9 kg)

♂♀ Miniature: both sexes
About 6 in (15 cm)
Up to 11 lb (5 kg)

Description This dog comes in two sizes (Standard and Miniature) and has a long, low-slung body. The skin is loose and the coat comes in three types: smooth, longhaired, and wirehaired. The coat comes in a range of colors.

Temperament An affectionate dog, it may be aggressive toward strangers. It may be difficult to house-train.

Grooming Brush all coat types with a bristle brush. Dry shampoo or bathe when necessary. Check ears regularly.

Exercise and feeding This dog loves regular walks, but discourage it from jumping. There are no secial feeding requirements. Do not overfeed or it will become fat and lazy.

Health problems It is prone to herniated disks in the back, obesity, and heart disease. It is also subject to diabetes, genetic eye diseases, and skin problems.

Standard longhaired dachshund

204 Whippet

Sensitive, gentle, high-strung

Regular brushing

Regular, moderate

Adapts well to urban living, but needs plenty of space

Not a good watchdog

♂ Male
18–20 in (46–51 cm)
20–22 lb (9–10 kg)

♀ Female
17–19 in (43–48 cm)
19–21 lb (9–10 kg)

Description The whippet has a delicate appearance. It has a fine, dense coat that comes in many colors, or in mixes. The muzzle is long and slender.

Temperament A docile pet, it is inclined to be nervous around children. Care must be taken not to break its spirit by being harsh or overbearing.

Grooming Groom with a bristle brush. Rub with a chamois to make the coat gleam. Bathe only when necessary.

Exercise and feeding Free running and long, brisk, daily walks are necessary. There are no special feeding requirements, but avoid giving it starchy or liquid food.

Health problems It is sensitive to cold and may get sunburned. Its bones are delicate and easy to break. It is also subject to genetic eye diseases, such as cataracts.

Basenji

 Intelligent, very independent

Weekly brushing

 Regular, vigorous

Well suited to urban living

 Poor watchdog

♂ Male
16–17 in (41–43 cm)
25–35 lb (11–16 kg)

♀ Female
15–16 in (38–41 cm)
20–30 lb (9–14 kg)

Description This compact, muscular dog has a distinctive trotting gait. Its loose, silky coat comes in combinations of white, tan, brindle, chestnut, and black. The tail is curled tightly over the back.

Temperament Alert and affectionate, this dog loves to play, and responds well to training. Provide plenty of chew toys and a secure fence—the basenji likes to climb.

Grooming Brush the shorthaired coat with a firm bristle brush and shampoo only when necessary.

Exercise and feeding Vigorous daily exercise is necessary. Green vegetables should be included in the diet.

Health problems This breed may suffer from kidney problems. It is also susceptible to progressive retinal atrophy and colitis (inflammation of the large intestine).

208 | Afghan hound

 Independent, lively, loving

 Extensive

 Regular, vigorous

 Adapts well to urban living, but needs plenty of space

 Not a good watchdog

♂ Male
27–29 in (69–74 cm)
55–65 lb (25–29 kg)

♀ Female
25–27 in (63–69 cm)
50–60 lb (23–27 kg)

Description This breed's coat is very long, straight, and silky. It comes in all colors and some combinations. The tail tip should curl in a complete ring. The gait is springy.

Temperament Although it is intelligent, the Afghan hound is not easy to train or handle. Owners need to establish a genuine relationship with their pet to succeed.

Grooming This dog's coat demands a lot of attention and must be brushed at least once a day. Dry shampoo when necessary and bathe once a month.

Exercise and feeding The Afghan hound must be allowed to run free in open spaces as well as have long daily walks. There are no special feeding requirements.

Health problems Generally a robust breed, it may suffer from hip dysplasia and eye problems.

WORKING DOGS

THIS GROUP WAS DEVELOPED FOR SPECIFIC
TASKS, SUCH AS GUARDING, DROVING
CATTLE, HAULING LOADS, AND RESCUE
WORK. THESE FEARLESS DOGS MAKE USEFUL
AND RELIABLE FAMILY FRIENDS.

212 Akita

 Brave, strong, alert

 Regular brushing

 Regular, moderate

 Adapts well to urban living, but needs plenty of space and exercise

 Good watchdog

♂ Male
21–24 in (53–61 cm)
90–110 lb (41–50 kg)

♀ Female
19–22 in (48–56 cm)
85–105 lb (38–48 kg)

Description This dog has a muscular body and a coat that comes in all colors, with clear markings. The tail is curled over the back. It has webbed feet and is a strong swimmer.

Temperament With diligent training, the Akita can make an excellent pet. It may be aggressive to other dogs. It is not suitable for first-time owners.

Grooming Its coarse, stiff coat sheds heavily twice a year and requires significant grooming. Brush with a firm bristle brush and bathe only when absolutely necessary.

Exercise and feeding It needs regular exercise, but avoid aggressive games. There are no special feeding requirements.

Health problems Illness is rare in this robust breed, but some are prone to hip dysplasia, thyroid problems, and genetic eye disease.

| Alaskan malamute

Gentle, friendly, good-natured

Brush twice weekly; more often when undercoat is molting

Regular, vigorous

Adapts well to urban living, but needs plenty of space

Ineffective watchdog

♂ Male
25–28 in (63–71 cm)
90–115 lb (41–52 kg)

♀ Female
23–26 in (58–66 cm)
85–110 lb (38–50 kg)

Description The face masking and underbody of this compact dog are always white, while the remaining coat may be light gray to black, gold to red, and liver. The plumed tail is carried over the back.

Temperament This dog is friendly, but it has a strong personality and a tendency to dominate. It needs early, consistent training from an experienced owner. It may become aggressive with other dogs.

Grooming Brush the coat twice a week, and more often during molting. Bathing is mostly unnecessary.

Exercise and feeding This dog needs a lot of exercise. It tends to wolf down its food, leading to bloat and obesity.

Health problems Subject to hip dysplasia, eye disease, and thyroid problems, it is also unsuited to hot climates.

216 Samoyed

Gentle, friendly, good-natured

Brush twice weekly; more when molting

Regular, robust

Adapts well to urban living, but needs plenty of space

Ineffective watchdog

♂ Male
20–22 in (51–56 cm)
45–55 lb (20–25 kg)

♀ Female
18–20 in (46–51 cm)
40–50 lb (18–23 kg)

Description A compact, muscular dog, its silver-tipped coat comes in white, biscuit, and cream. Its thick, perky tail curls over the back and to one side.

Temperament The Samoyed is independent and strong, so training should begin at an early age. It willingly adapts to family life, and loves children.

Grooming It sheds heavily, so brush regularly. Dry shampoo from time to time. Bathing is mostly unnecessary.

Exercise and feeding This dog needs robust daily exercise. There are no special feeding requirements, but the Samoyed is partial to fish.

Health problems It is particularly prone to hip dysplasia, skin and eye problems, and diabetes. This dog does not tolerate hot climates.

Siberian husky

 Playful, friendly, good-natured

 Brush twice weekly; more when molting

 Regular, vigorous

 Adapts well to urban living, but needs plenty of space

 Ineffective watchdog

 ♂ Male
21–23 in (53–58 cm)
45–60 lb (20–27 kg)

♀ Female
20–22 in (51–56 cm)
35–50 lb (16–23 kg)

Description The face mask and underbody of this strong, compact dog are usually white. The remaining coat can be any color. Mismatched eyes are common.

Temperament An affectionate pet, this dog is dependable around children. It may be hard to train and needs an experienced owner.

Grooming The undercoat needs extra care during molting season. Dry shampoo from time to time. Bathing is mostly unnecessary. Clip the nails regularly.

Exercise and feeding It needs regular exercise, but less in warm weather. It needs less food than might be expected.

Health problems The breed is subject to hip dysplasia as well as skin, thyroid, and occasional eye problems. It is unsuited to life in hot climates.

Saint Bernard

 Placid, affectionate, loyal

 Frequent brushing

 Regular, moderate

 Well suited to urban living if given plenty of space and exercise

 Good watchdog

♂ Male
27 in (69 cm) or more
From 172 lb (80 kg)

♀ Female
25 in (63 cm) or more
From 160 lb (72 kg)

Description Smooth- and rough-coated varieties are available. Both types come in white, with tan, mahogany, red, brindle, and black markings in various combinations.

Temperament Dignified, reliable, and highly intelligent, this dog is good with children and easy to train.

Grooming Brush more when it is shedding. Bathe only when necessary. Keep the jowls and chest clean of drool, and clean the eyes and ears regularly. Keep nails trimmed.

Exercise and feeding Give an adult dog long daily walks, but restrict a puppy to short walks. This breed is susceptible to bloat, so give it two or three small meals a day.

Health problems It is particularly prone to hip dysplasia and heart disease. It may also suffer from epilepsy, skin problems, and an eye condition that causes weeping.

Great Pyrenees

Calm, gentle, dignified

Regular brushing

Regular, extensive

Adapts well to urban living, but needs plenty of space and exercise

Very good watchdog

Male
25–32 in (63–81 cm)
100–130 lb (45–59 kg)

♀
Female
23–30 in (58–76 cm)
90–120 lb (41–54 kg)

Description This is a very large, muscular dog, with a coarse waterproof coat of solid white, or white with patches of tan, pale yellow, or wolf-gray.

Temperament Although it is calm and intelligent, this breed must receive consistent training while young and small. It does not reach maturity until two years of age.

Grooming The outer coat does not mat, so a couple of brushings a week (more when molting) are all it needs. Bathe only when necessary.

Exercise and feeding This breed needs plenty of exercise. There are no specific feeding requirements, although it has a relatively small appetite.

Health problems It may suffer from eye diseases, deafness, and orthopedic problems, such as hip dysplasia.

Newfoundland

Sweet, intelligent, protective

Daily brushing

Regular, moderate

Adapts well to urban living, but needs plenty of space

Good watchdog

♂ Male
27–29 in (69–74 cm)
138–150 lb (63–68 kg)

♀ Female
25–27 in (63–69 cm)
110–120 lb (50–54 kg)

Description The dog's thick, coarse, double coat comes in blacks, browns, or black with white markings. This water-loving breed has webbing between its toes.

Temperament Renowned for its gentleness with children, the Newfoundland is also adaptable, loyal, and courageous, with great strength and endurance. Rather than bark, it uses its body to deter strangers. It is easy to train and house-train.

Grooming Use a hard brush every day, and take extra care during molting. Bathe only when absolutely necessary.

Exercise and feeding This dog will benefit from moderate exercise and swimming. There are no special feeding requirements, but do not overfeed.

Health problems It is prone to heart and orthopedic diseases. The dog is also unsuited to hot climates.

| Mastiff

 Reliable, valiant, but can be aggressive

Regular brushing

 Regular, moderate

 Adapts well to urban living, but needs plenty of space

 Outstanding watchdog

♂ Male
From 30 in (76 cm)
From about 160 lb (72 kg)

♀ Female
From 27 in (69 cm)
From about 150 lb (68 kg)

Description This powerful dog has a dense, flat-lying coat that comes in shades of apricot, silver, fawn, or darker fawn brindle. The muzzle and nose are black.

Temperament When properly handled, the mastiff is docile, good-natured, and loyal. An exceptional guard dog, the mastiff must be trained with firm kindness.

Grooming Brush the coarse coat with a firm bristle brush. Bathe or dry shampoo when necessary.

Exercise and feeding Inclined to be lazy, the mastiff will be fitter and happier if given regular exercise. It is best to keep it leashed in public. Feed two or three small meals a day to avoid bloat.

Health problems It is prone to bloat, and may suffer from hip dysplasia and genetic eye diseases.

| Rottweiler

Brave, intelligent, formidable

Weekly brushing

Regular, vigorous

Adapts well to urban living, but needs plenty of exercise

Excellent watchdog

♂ Male
25–27 in (63–69 cm)
100–135 lb (45–61 kg)

♀ Female
23–25 in (58–63 cm)
90–120 lb (41–54 kg)

Description This muscular dog has a thick coat with a fine undercoat. It is always black with rich tan markings. The tail is docked at the first joint.

Temperament Prized for its aggression and guarding abilities, this dog can, with kind, firm, and consistent handling, also be a loving pet. Training and socialization must begin young to curb its nature.

Grooming A firm bristle brush will keep the coat glossy. Bathe only when necessary.

Exercise and feeding Provide lots of work and exercise, but avoid aggressive games like tug-of-war. There are no special feeding requirements, but do not overfeed pups.

Health problems It is prone to orthopedic, skin, and eye diseases, bleeding disorders, diabetes, and paralysis.

Gentle, loyal, affectionate

Daily brushing

Regular, moderate

Adapts well to urban living, but needs plenty of space

Very good watchdog

♂ Male
30–32 in (76–81 cm)
100–125 lb (45–57 kg)

♀ Female
28–30 in (71–76 cm)
90–105 lb (41–48 kg)

Description This large, muscular dog has a dense, sleek coat that comes in fawn, black, blue, striped brindle, and harlequin (white with black patches).

Temperament This dog is well behaved when properly socialized, but it can be aggressive with other dogs. It is usually even tempered around its family, children included.

Grooming Use a firm bristle brush daily and dry shampoo when necessary. Keep nails trimmed.

Exercise and feeding This dog needs plenty of exercise, but avoid aggressive games. It has special nutritional needs during its growing period, which can last 20 months. Feed two or three small meals a day to avoid bloat.

Health problems It is prone to hip dysplasia and genetic heart problems. Bone cancer and bloat are also common.

Fun-loving, protective, loyal

 Daily brushing

 Regular, vigorous

 Adapts well to urban living, but needs plenty of space

Excellent watchdog

♂ Male
22–24 in (56–61 cm)
60–70 lb (27–32 kg)

♀ Female
21–23 in (53–58 cm)
55–65 lb (25–29 kg)

Description This is a compact and powerful dog with a shiny coat that comes in fawn, brindle, and various shades of red, all with white markings. The tail is usually docked.

Temperament This dog should be handled by a strong adult. Training should start young and be consistent and firm. It is reliable with children and intensely loyal to its family, but may be aggressive with other dogs.

Grooming Brush the smooth, shorthaired coat with a firm bristle brush and bathe only when necessary.

Exercise and feeding This playful, athletic dog needs long, brisk walks and lots of daily exercise. Feed two or three small meals a day to avoid bloat.

Health problems A short-lived breed, it is subject to heart disease, cancer, stroke, and skin and breathing problems.

234 | Doberman pinscher

Intelligent, loyal, and fearless; may be aggressive

Regular brushing

Regular, vigorous

Adapts to urban living if given enough space and exercise

Superb watchdog

♂ Male
25–27 in (63–69 cm)
55–75 lb (25–34 kg)

♀ Female
23–26 in (58–66 cm)
50–70 lb (23–32 kg)

Description An elegant, muscular dog, the Doberman has a close-fitting coat that comes in black, or black and tan; blue-gray, red, and fawn also occur.

Temperament This dog needs firm and determined training from puppyhood. It is easy to train, but should always be supervised around children.

Grooming The smooth coat does not shed much. Use a bristle brush and bathe only when necessary.

Exercise and feeding It needs plenty of daily exercise. Feed two or three small meals a day to avoid bloat.

Health problems It is prone to heart disease, diabetes, liver dysfunctions, von Willebrand's disease, eye problems, and orthopedic problems that include hip dysplasia. Do not expose it to extreme cold.

TERRIERS

MOSTLY SMALL DOGS WITH SHORT LEGS
AND POWERFUL JAWS, TERRIERS ARE QUICK,
TENACIOUS, AND BRAVE. THEY ARE VERY
INQUISITIVE AND INTELLIGENT, AND MAKE
PLAYFUL, ENGAGING COMPANIONS.

| Cairn terrier

Frisky, plucky, companionable

Regular brushing

Regular, moderate

Ideal for apartment living

Good watchdog

♂ Male
10–13 in (25–33 cm)
14–18 lb (6–8 kg)

♀ Female
9–12 in (23–30 cm)
13–17 lb (6–8 kg)

Description This compact dog has a thick undercoat and a weather-resistant outer coat that comes in red, sandy, gray, cream, wheaten, brindle, black, pure white, or black and tan.

Temperament Intelligent and easily trained, this breed is devoted to its owner almost to the point of jealousy. It may bark excessively, and some are incorrigible diggers.

Grooming Brush several times a week. Bathe monthly and brush coat while it dries. Trim around the eyes and ears with blunt-nosed scissors and clip the nails regularly.

Exercise and feeding This dog will exercise itself in a fenced garden. If you live in an apartment, a daily walk will be necessary. There are no special feeding requirements.

Health problems It is prone to skin allergies, dislocating kneecaps, and hereditary eye diseases.

Scottish terrier

 Happy, brave, loyal

 Regular brushing

 Regular, moderate

 Ideal for apartment living

 Very good watchdog

♂ Male
10–11 in (25–28 cm)
19–23 lb (9–10 kg)

♀ Female
9–10 in (23–25 cm)
18–22 lb (8–10 kg)

Description Strong, active, and agile despite short legs, this dog has a rough, weather-resistant coat that comes in black, steel, iron-gray, wheaten, or brindle of any color.

Temperament Bold and self-possessed, the Scottie can also be stubborn and should be handled firmly. It is inclined to snap, and likes to dig and go wandering.

Grooming Regular brushing is needed, especially when molting. The dog should be trimmed twice a year.

Exercise and feeding In a yard of reasonable size, the dog will exercise itself. It will enjoy walks and play sessions. Beware of overfeeding or it will become fat and lazy.

Health problems It is prone to von Willebrand's disease, skin allergies, jawbone disorders, and "Scottie cramp," which makes walking difficult.

| West Highland white terrier

 Adaptable, bright, friendly

 Daily brushing

 Regular, gentle

 Ideal for apartment living, but needs regular exercise

Good watchdog

♂ Male
10–12 in (25–30 cm)
15–18 lb (7–8 kg)

♀ Female
9–11 in (23–28 cm)
13–16 lb (6–7 kg)

Description A sturdy terrier with a harsh, all-white double coat and bright, dark eyes. The ears are small, pointed, and erect. The tail is carried jauntily and should not be docked.

Temperament This dog loves company and is suited to homes with older children. Strong and brave, it is easier to train than most terriers, but will also bark and dig a lot.

Grooming Brush several times a week to minimize the need for bathing. Trim around the eyes and ears. Trim the coat every four months and strip it twice a year.

Exercise and feeding This dog enjoys daily walks and games. There are no special feeding requirements.

Health problems It is prone to skin allergies, copper toxicosis, jawbone disorders, hernias, and deterioration of the hip joint.

Miniature schnauzer

 Playful, smart, stubborn

 Daily brushing

 Regular, moderate

 Ideal for apartment living, but needs plenty of exercise

Excellent watchdog

♂ Male
12–14 in (30–36 cm)
11–18 lb (5–8 kg)

♀ Female
11–13 in (28–33 cm)
10–15 lb (5–7 kg)

Description This strong, angular dog has a harsh, wiry double coat that comes in salt and pepper or any solid color. It has thick, prominent eyebrows and a mustache. The tail is usually docked.

Temperament This excitable dog will bark and dig, but is reliable and affectionate. It may be scrappy with other dogs.

Grooming Groom daily with a short wire brush. The dog should be clipped twice a year. Trim around the eyes and ears, and clean the whiskers after meals.

Exercise and feeding This lively dog enjoys brisk, daily walks. There are no special feeding requirements.

Health problems It may suffer from von Willebrand's disease, kidney and bladder stones, liver disease, diabetes, and eye and skin disorders.

| Airedale terrier

 Reliable, loyal, lively

 Regular brushing

 Regular, moderate

 Adapts well to urban living, but needs plenty of exercise

 Good watchdog

♂ Male
23–24 in (58–61 cm)
40–50 lb (18–23 kg)

♀ Female
22–23 in (56–58 cm)
40–45 lb (18–20 kg)

Description This strong dog has a stiff, wiry coat that comes in a combination of dark grizzle or black with red and tan markings. It has a beard, mustache, and bushy eyebrows. The tail is usually docked.

Temperament Intelligent and faithful, this dog loves children. It has a strong personality and needs firm handling. The Airedale is an incorrigible digger.

Grooming Remove the dead hair from the coat with a stiff bristle brush and bathe only when necessary.

Exercise and feeding This dog is easily bored, so it needs plenty of exercise. Extra oil in the diet is recommended if it suffers from a dry, itchy skin.

Health problems It is prone to von Willebrand's disease, hip dysplasia, gastroenteritis, and eye problems.

Border terrier

 Energetic, affectionate, loyal

 Minimal

 Regular, vigorous

 Ideal for urban and apartment living, but needs plenty of exercise

 Good watchdog

 Male
13–16 in (33–41 cm)
13–16 lb (6–7 kg)

♀ Female
11–14 in (28–36 cm)
11–14 lb (5–6 kg)

Description This dog's wiry double coat comes in reds, blue and tan, grizzle and tan, or wheaten. Its muzzle and ears are usually dark, and its head is described as otter-like.

Temperament Reliable and intelligent, this breed is easily trained and obedient. It may hunt your cat and be aggressive with other dogs.

Grooming The coat needs little grooming. Clip out knots and brush occasionally. Bathe only when necessary.

Exercise and feeding The border terrier has great vitality and stamina. If bored it can become destructive, so provide plenty of exercise. There are no special feeding requirements.

Health problems This dog is hardy. It has few genetic problems, but may suffer from dislocating kneecaps.

Determined, fearless, playful

 Regular brushing

 Regular, moderate

 Adapts well to urban living, needs plenty of space to exercise

 Good watchdog

♂ Male
15–19 in (38–48 cm)
60–70 lb (27–32 kg)

♀ Female
15–19 in (38–48 cm)
60–70 lb (27–32 kg)

Description A thick-set, muscular dog, it has a long, flat, curving head and small eyes. Its coat comes in white or black, brindle, red, fawn, and tricolor with white markings.

Temperament When socialized and trained it can be a devoted companion that is usually sweet-natured and gentle. It will fight with other dogs.

Grooming Brush its smooth, short coat with a firm bristle brush once a week, and bathe as necessary.

Exercise and feeding The bull terrier needs regular exercise to keep it in good health. Do not overfeed.

Health problems It may suffer from zinc deficiency and skin allergies. White dogs may be born deaf and be susceptible to heart disease, skin inflammations, and sunburn. Colored dogs are not so prone to these conditions.

| American Staffordshire terrier

 Stoic, reliable, courageous

 Daily brushing

 Regular, moderate

 Adapts well to urban living, but needs plenty of exercise

Excellent watchdog

♂ Male
17–19 in (43–48 cm)
40–50 lb (18–23 kg)

♀ Female
16–18 in (41–46 cm)
35–45 lb (16–20 kg)

Description This broad-chested, muscular dog has a smooth, short coat that comes in white or solid reds, fawn, brindle, black or blue, or any of these colors with white.

Temperament It is a brave and tenacious fighter if provoked, and needs firm, kind training to control this instinct. It is generally gentle and kind with people.

Grooming Use a firm bristle brush every day, and bathe or dry shampoo as necessary. A rub with a piece of toweling or chamois will make the coat gleam.

Exercise and feeding This terrier must have plenty of regular exercise. There are no special feeding requirements, but do not overfeed as it is inclined to become fat and lazy.

Health problems While not long-lived, it is relatively free of genetic weaknesses. It may develop cataracts.

Intelligent, loyal, brave

 Regular brushing

 Regular, vigorous

 Adapts to urban living, but needs plenty of exercise

Excellent watchdog

♂ Male
16–19 in (41–48 cm)
25–30 lb (11–14 kg)

♀ Female
15–18 in (38–46 cm)
23–28 lb (10–13 kg)

Description This game little terrier has a hard, short, wiry coat that comes in solid red, yellow-red, or red-wheaten colors. The tail is docked to three-fourths of its length.

Temperament It is sociable with people and devoted to its owner, but will fight other dogs. Although attentive and easy to train, it needs thorough socialization as a pup.

Grooming The double coat rarely sheds. Brush regularly with a stiff bristle brush and strip loose, dead hair weekly with a fine-toothed comb. Bathe only when necessary.

Exercise and feeding This dog needs plenty of regular exercise. There are no special feeding requirements.

Health problems The Irish terrier is a robust dog, but is susceptible to an hereditary urinary problem, and foot and eye diseases.

TOY DOGS

BRED PRIMARILY FOR THE PLEASURE OF THEIR
OWNERS, TOY DOGS HAVE PERSONALITIES IN
INVERSE PROPORTION TO THEIR TINY BODIES.
THEY ARE UNQUESTIONABLY LOYAL AND
MANY MAKE COURAGEOUS WATCHDOGS.

258 | Chihuahua

 Affectionate, alert, playful

 Gentle, regular brushing

 Regular, gentle

 Ideal for apartment living

 Poor watchdog

♂ Male
6–9 in (15–23 cm)
2–6 lb (1–3 kg)

♀ Female
6–8 in (15–20 cm)
2–6 lb (1–3 kg)

Description This is the world's smallest breed. There are two distinct coat types: smooth and short, or long. Every color and combination occurs.

Temperament This intelligent and lively dog is intensely loyal. It may be difficult to house-train. When frightened it may bite; excessive barking can also be a problem.

Grooming Brush the short coat regularly and the long coat daily. Bathe both types once a month.

Exercise and feeding It will benefit from short daily walks. A body harness is safer than a collar and leash. Feed small amounts twice a day.

Health problems This long-lived breed suffers from collapsing trachea, dislocating kneecaps, heart disease, and eye, tooth, and gum problems.

Longhaired chihuahua

Toy poodle

 Very intelligent, excitable

 Comb and brush daily

 Regular, gentle

 Ideal for apartment living

 Very good watchdog for its size

♂ Male
Up to 11 in (28 cm)
6–9 lb (3–4 kg)

♀ Female
Up to 11 in (28 cm)
6–9 lb (3–4 kg)

Description This active dog has a dense, woolly coat of springy curls that comes in solid red, white, cream, blue, brown, apricot, black, and silver.

Temperament It is sensitive, highly responsive, and easy to train, but it can be snappish. It is demanding of affection and may bark a lot.

Grooming The toy poodle must be bathed regularly and clipped every six to eight weeks. Nails should be kept short; ears and teeth should be cleaned and checked regularly.

Exercise and feeding This dog is happier and healthier if given opportunities to run free and play. There are no special feeding requirements.

Health problems It is prone to epilepsy, dislocating kneecaps, heart and eye diseases, cysts, and diabetes.

| Maltese

 Even-tempered, affectionate

 Regular, extensive; be careful with soft coat

 Regular, gentle

 Ideal for apartment living

Adequate watchdog

♂ Male
8–10 in (20–25 cm)
6–10 lb (3–5 kg)

♀ Female
8–10 in (20–25 cm)
6–10 lb (3–5 kg)

Description This dog's silky coat falls long and straight, parting along the spine and concealing the short legs completely. It is always white. The tail arches over the back.

Temperament Intelligent and easy to train, the Maltese is generally good-natured, but can be snappy when handled roughly. It will bark if strangers are about.

Grooming Daily grooming is essential. Check and wipe the eyes and beard daily to prevent staining. The fringe is often tied in a topknot. Bathe or dry shampoo regularly.

Exercise and feeding This dog enjoys walking and playing. Avoid overfeeding or pandering to a fussy eater.

Health problems The Maltese is generally hardy, but is subject to eye and joint problems, tooth and gum conditions, hypoglycemia, and sunburn.

Friendly, playful, independent

 Extensive

 Regular, gentle

 Ideal for apartment living

 Adequate watchdog

 ♂ Male
Up to 11 in (28 cm)
10–18 lb (5–8 kg)

♀ Female
Up to 11 in (28 cm)
10–18 lb (5–8 kg)

Description This little dog has a long body and short legs. It has a thick, long, luxuriant coat that can be any color, but a white blaze on the forehead and a white tail tip are very desirable.

Temperament The gentle, loyal shih tzu makes friends readily and is easily trained. It does not snap or bark a lot.

Grooming Daily combing and brushing of the soft coat, and cleaning of the beard, is essential. Ears and feet need to be checked and cleaned regularly. Bathe monthly.

Exercise and feeding This dog needs to be encouraged to exercise. Do not overfeed, or it quickly will get fat.

Health problems Its prominent eyes are prone to injury and dryness. It is subject to respiratory conditions, ear infections, heatstroke, and kidney, joint, and dental problems.

Pomeranian

 Lively, inquisitive, friendly

 Frequent brushing

 Regular, gentle

 Ideal for apartment living

 Good watchdog despite its size

♂ Male
7–9 in (18–23 cm)
3–5 lb (1.5–2 kg)

♀ Female
7–9 in (18–23 cm)
4–6 lb (2–3 kg)

Description This breed looks like a walking powderpuff of dense black, gray, blue, orange, cream, shaded sable, or particolored hair. It has a foxlike face and a spectacular tail.

Temperament Easily trained, this bold, extroverted dog is a good watchdog. Its barking may become a problem if not curbed from an early age.

Grooming Frequent brushing of the long double coat, and the tail, is recommended. Dry shampoo when necessary. Clean the eyes and ears daily, and check teeth regularly.

Exercise and feeding A small play area will suffice for exercise. There are no special feeding requirements.

Health problems It is subject to diabetes, dislocating knees, and eye and heart problems. Tooth loss may occur if they are not cared for.

Pekingese

 Intelligent, devoted, determined

 Special care is needed

 Regular, gentle

Ideal for apartment living

Excellent watchdog for its size

♂ Male
7–10 in (18–25 cm)
7–11 lb (3–5 kg)

♀ Female
7–10 in (18–25 cm)
8–13 lb (4–6 kg)

Description Its flowing coat comes in all colors except albino and liver. The flat face has a dark, wrinkled muzzle and the drooping ears are heart-shaped.

Temperament Affectionate with its owner but aloof with strangers, this dog can be hard to train and house-train. The Pekingese is better for homes without young children.

Grooming Daily grooming of the long, straight coat is essential. Dry shampoo regularly. Clean the face and eyes daily and check the feet for trapped debris.

Exercise and feeding This dog should be encouraged to exercise. It quickly will become obese if overfed.

Health problems The Pekingese is subject to breathing problems and skin infections. The prominent eyes are sensitive and prone to corneal ulcers and injury.

Yorkshire terrier

 Courageous, clever, feisty

 Daily, extensive

 Regular, gentle

 Ideal for apartment living

 Good watchdog despite its size

♂ Male
7–9 in (18–23 cm)
4–7 lb (2–3 kg)

♀ Female
7–9 in (18–23 cm)
3–7 lb (1.5–3 kg)

Description The long, fine, silky single coat parts along the spine and falls straight down on either side. It is steel-blue on the body and tail, and tan elsewhere. The tail is usually docked to half its length.

Temperament This alert, tiny terrier is very loyal. It tends to bark a lot and can be snappish. It is unsuitable for a home with young children.

Grooming Daily combing and brushing, and regular shampooing, are necessary to keep the hair in top condition.

Exercise and feeding This dog does not need much exercise. Meat intake should be restricted, and fussy eaters should not be indulged.

Health problems It is prone to eye, hip, and gum problems, collapsing tracheas, and dislocating knees.

| Pug

 Smart, sociable, mischievous

 Daily brushing

Regular, moderate

 Ideal for apartment living
if given enough exercise

 Good watchdog

♂ Male
12–14 in (30–36 cm)
13–20 lb (6–9 kg)

 ♀ Female
10–12 in (25–30 cm)
13–18 lb (6–8 kg)

Description This strong dog has a square, thickset body and a sleek coat that comes in fawn, apricot, silver, and black, all with a black muzzle and ears. The tail lies in a tight curl (or sometimes a double curl) on its back.

Temperament An intelligent dog, the pug is playful and affectionate, and not inclined to snap.

Grooming The soft, short coat needs only a weekly brushing and does not shed much. Clean the face regularly.

Exercise and feeding The pug enjoys energetic games. It loves to eat, but do not overfeed or it will become obese.

Health problems Its muzzle contributes to breathing problems. It may suffer allergies, and it is stressed by both hot and cold weather. Its prominent eyes are prone to injury. The tail and face are susceptible to skin-fold infections.

Brave, playful, inquisitive

Daily brushing

Regular, gentle

Ideal for apartments, but barking can be a problem

Excellent watchdog for its size

♂ Male
10–12 in (25–30 cm)
8–10 lb (4–5 kg)

♀ Female
10–11 in (25–28 cm)
8–9 lb (about 4 kg)

Description This dog's smooth, hard coat comes in black, blue, and chocolate, all with tan markings on the face and matching patches on the chest and above the eyes. Solid reds are also seen. The tail is usually docked short.

Temperament This dog will bark and nip at intruders. It is not easy to train and is unsuited to homes with small children. It also may be aggressive with other dogs.

Grooming The coat is easy to groom. Use a firm bristle brush or wipe with a chamois. Bathe only when necessary.

Exercise and feeding Needs regular exercise. Ensure that the yard has a high enough fence to foil an escape attempt. There are no special feeding requirements.

Health problems A robust breed, it is subject to eye and joint problems, and does not tolerate cold weather.

276 | Chinese crested

 Lively, gentle, devoted

 Powderpuff needs daily brushing; hairless needs frequent bathing

 Regular, gentle

 Ideal for apartment living

 Not a good watchdog

 ♂ Male
9–13 in (23–33 cm)
Up to 12 lb (5 kg)

♀ Female
9–13 in (23–33 cm)
Up to 12 lb (5 kg)

Description This breed comes in two body types (one is heavier than the other) and with two varieties of coat. One type of coat is hairless except for its head, ears, tail, and feet, and the other (called the powderpuff) is totally covered with soft, silky hair.

Temperament This dog craves constant companionship. It loves children and the company of other animals. It may be difficult to house-train.

Grooming The hairless variety needs weekly brushing and bathing. The powderpuff needs daily grooming.

Exercise and feeding This dog enjoys exercise. There are no special feeding requirements, but do not overfeed.

Health problems Both varieties are prone to eye and skin conditions. The hairless variety is prone to sunburn.

Hairless Chinese crested

THE MEMBERS OF THIS GROUP DO NOT FIT NEATLY INTO THE OTHER BREED CATEGORIES. THEY HAVE LITTLE IN COMMON, BUT THEY ARE SOME OF THE MOST BEAUTIFUL, INTELLIGENT, AND POPULAR PETS TODAY.

280 Bichon frise

 Charming, friendly, playful

 Extensive

 Regular, gentle

 Ideal for apartment living

 Good watchdog

 Male
9–11 in (23–28 cm)
11–16 lb (5–7 kg)

♀ Female
9–11 in (23–28 cm)
11–16 lb (5–7 kg)

Description This sturdy little dog has a puffy white coat, sometimes with cream or apricot markings. The eyes and nose are large, round, and dark.

Temperament Confident and gregarious, this breed is intelligent and easy to train. It is generally even-tempered and sociable among family and strangers.

Grooming Daily brushing is essential. The curly hair is trimmed and brushed out to a soft cloud. Trim around the eyes and ears, and clean the eyes. Bathe once a month.

Exercise and feeding Play will take care of most of its needs, but the bichon frise loves to walk and romp in the open. There are no special feeding requirements.

Health problems It may suffer from epilepsy and dislocating kneecaps. It is also prone to eye problems.

| Dalmatian

 Sensitive, spirited, energetic

 Daily brushing

 Regular, vigorous

 Adapts to urban living, but needs plenty of exercise

Good watchdog

♂ Male
22–25 in (56–63 cm)
50–65 lb (23–29 kg)

♀ Female
21–24 in (53–61 cm)
45–60 lb (20–27 kg)

Description This lean, well-muscled breed is born with a white coat and develops the black or liver-colored spots during the first year.

Temperament A boisterous dog, it loves children. It is sensitive, so needs patient training and firm handling.

Grooming This breed is a heavy shedder. Daily brushing is required. Bathe only when necessary.

Exercise and feeding Athletic by nature, the dalmatian is not an ideal apartment dog unless it is exercised several times a day. When bored, it becomes destructive. Be careful not to overfeed as it easily becomes obese.

Health problems It has problems with hip dysplasia, urinary bladder stones, skin allergies, and sunburn. It is also prone to deafness.

284 | Boston terrier

Playful, devoted, fearless

Daily cleaning

Regular, moderate

Ideal for apartment living

Excellent watchdog

♂ Male
11–15 in (28–38 cm)
15–25 lb (7–11 kg)

♀ Female
11–15 in (28–38 cm)
15–25 lb (7–11 kg)

Description This well-muscled dog has a short, wide muzzle; prominent, wide-set eyes; and short, erect ears. The coat is black or brindle, with white markings.

Temperament Affectionate to people and reliable with children, this dog may scrap with other dogs. Intelligent and easy to train, it may become anxious if left alone.

Grooming The shorthaired coat is easy to groom with a firm bristle brush. Use a chamois to wipe the face every day, and clean the prominent eyes carefully.

Exercise and feeding Regular walks or play in a yard will keep it fit. There are no special feeding requirements.

Health problems This short-faced dog may develop breathing problems when stressed. Heart conditions, skin tumors, eye injuries, and skin-fold infections are common.

286 | Bulldog

Reliable, calm, sweet

Regular brushing

Regular, moderate

Adapts well to urban living

Very good watchdog

♂ Male
14–16 in (36–41 cm)
55–70 lb (25–32 kg)

♀ Female
12–14 in (30–36 cm)
48–60 lb (22–27 kg)

Description With its stocky legs and compact, muscular body, the bulldog's gait is really a waddle. The coat comes in reds, fawn, brindle, or fallow, or white pied with these.

Temperament This is among the gentlest of breeds and is a good playmate for children.

Grooming Comb and brush the short, fine coat, and bathe only when necessary. Wipe the face clean every day.

Exercise and feeding The bulldog needs regular, but not overly strenuous, exercise. Be careful not to overfeed as it easily becomes obese. May be possessive of its food.

Health problems This short-lived breed suffers eye and heart problems and skin infections. Its short muzzle and narrow nostrils cause breathing difficulties and heatstroke. It is also stressed by exertion and hot or cold weather.

Standard poodle

 Very clever, responsive, fun

 Comb and brush daily

 Regular, moderate

 Ideal for apartment living, but needs plenty of exercise

Very good watchdog

♂ Male
15–24 in (38–61 cm)
45–70 lb (20–32 kg)

♀ Female
15–22 in (38–56 cm)
45–60 lb (20–27 kg)

Description This active dog has a dense, woolly coat that comes in white, black, cream, brown, apricot, silver, and blue. The hair does not shed. The tail is usually docked.

Temperament This intelligent breed is exuberant and independent. It is particularly easy to house-train, and makes a great playmate for children.

Grooming The dog must be bathed regularly and clipped every six to eight weeks from puppyhood. Check the ears regularly for infection and for mites, and keep teeth clean.

Exercise and feeding The poodle loves to swim, run, and play. To prevent bloat, feed two or three small meals a day and avoid exercise after meals.

Health problems This long-lived breed is subject to bloat, eye diseases, allergies, cysts, and other skin conditions.

290 | Lhasa apso

 Clever, devoted, very alert

 Daily, extensive

 Regular, gentle to moderate

 Ideally suited to apartment living

 Very good watchdog

♂ Male
10–11 in (25–28 cm)
14–18 lb (6–8 kg)

♀ Female
9–10 in (23–25 cm)
12–16 lb (5–7 kg)

Description This dog's long, coarse coat covers its entire body, including its eyes, ears, and feet. It also has a beard and a mustache. The coat can be gold, cream, honey, smoke, slate, or browns, or particolors of black, white, or brown.

Temperament Adaptable, playful, and affectionate, this is a one-person dog, which is better suited to families with older children. It can be stubborn and needs firm handling.

Grooming Needs daily combing and brushing. Clean the feet, eyes, and ears regularly. Dry shampoo it as necessary, but bathe no more than three times a year.

Exercise and feeding This dog loves to run and play. There are no special feeding requirements.

Health problems It may suffer from kidney conditions, ear infections, eye injuries, and blocked tear ducts.

Chow chow

 Reserved, independent;
a one-person dog

 Regular brushing

 Regular, moderate

 Adapts to urban living,
but needs space

 Very good watchdog

♂ Male
18–23 in (46–56 cm)
50–65 lb (23–29 kg)

♀ Female
18–22 in (46–53 cm)
45–60 lb (20–27 kg)

Description This dog's two distinctive features are its blue-black tongue and its almost straight hindlegs, which make its walk rather stilted. Its double coat comes in solid black, red, fawn, cream, blue, or white. The ears are small and rounded, and there is a huge ruff behind the head.

Temperament This strong-willed dog can be difficult to train. Suspicious of strangers, it can be very territorial.

Grooming The coat sheds heavily and should be brushed three times a week. Dry shampoo when necessary.

Exercise and feeding The dog can be lazy and will benefit from a daily walk. There are no special feeding requirements, but do not overfeed.

Health problems It is prone to eczema, joint problems, and eye diseases. The breed is unsuited to hot climates.

Shar-pei

 Independent, intensely loyal

 Regular brushing

 Regular, moderate

 Adapts well to urban living, but needs plenty of space

 Good watchdog

♂ Male
18–20 in (46–51 cm)
40–55 lb (18–25 kg)

♀ Female
18–20 in (46–51 cm)
40–55 lb (18–25 kg)

Description There are two varieties of shar-pei: a heavily wrinkled dog with a large head, and a smaller-headed dog with tighter-looking skin. The coat comes in red, fawn, cream, apricot, and black. The dog has a blue-black tongue.

Temperament The shar-pei is a one-person dog with a strong guarding instinct. It can be aggressive with strangers and other animals, and needs firm training from an early age.

Grooming Regular brushing will keep the unusual coat in good condition. Dry shampoo or bathe when necessary.

Exercise and feeding Daily walks and an occasional run are beneficial. There are no special feeding requirements.

Health problems The shar-pei suffers from chronic skin problems and inflammatory bowel disease. It may also need corrective eye surgery.

296 | Shiba Inu

 Energetic, friendly, loyal

 Regular brushing

 Regular, moderate

 Ideal for urban or apartment living, but needs plenty of exercise

 Good watchdog

 Male
14–16 in (36–41 cm)
20–30 lb (9–14 kg)

 Female
13–15 in (33–38 cm)
18–28 lb (8–13 kg)

Description Agile and well-proportioned, the Shiba Inu has a strong body and alert bearing. The waterproof, all-weather coat comes in red, sable, or black and tan, with pale shadings on the legs, belly, chest, face, and tail.

Temperament Lively and good-natured, this intelligent dog can be difficult to train. It is extremely sociable, but can be aggressive to unfamiliar dogs. It loves to dig and climb.

Grooming Groom the coarse, stiff double coat with a firm bristle brush. Bathe only when absolutely necessary, as this strips the coat's waterproofing.

Exercise and feeding This active dog needs lots of exercise. There are no special feeding requirements.

Health problems The breed is generally hardy and healthy, with few genetic weaknesses.

HERDING DOGS

HERDING DOGS HAVE BEEN USED FOR CENTURIES TO ASSEMBLE, DRIVE, AND RETRIEVE LIVESTOCK AND TO PROTECT IT FROM THIEVES AND PREDATORS. THESE DOGS ARE AGILE AND INTELLIGENT.

300 | Pembroke Welsh corgi

Affectionate, loyal, independent

Regular brushing

Regular, gentle

Ideal for apartment living, but needs plenty of exercise

Very good watchdog

♂ Male
10–12 in (25–30 cm)
20–24 lb (9–11 kg)

♀ Female
10–12 in (25–30 cm)
18–22 lb (8–10 kg)

Description The long, powerful body is set on short, well-boned legs. Its coat comes in red, sable, fawn, tan, and black, all with or without white. The tail may be docked.

Temperament This clever dog is wary of strangers. It is easy to train and house-train. It loves children, but does have a tendency to nip people, as this is how it herds.

Grooming The thick, soft, water-resistant coat sheds heavily twice a year and drops hair all year round. Use a firm bristle brush every week and bathe only when necessary.

Exercise and feeding This dog should be encouraged to run and play. Do not overfeed as it will become fat and lazy.

Health problems Its short legs and long back make it prone to slipped spinal disks. It may also suffer inherited eye disorders, bleeding disorders, and hip dysplasia.

| Australian shepherd

Keen, obedient, energetic

Minimal

Regular, vigorous

Adapts well to urban living, but needs plenty of space and exercise

Good watchdog

♂ Male
19–23 in (48–58 cm)
40–70 lb (18–32 kg)

♀ Female
18–22 in (46–56 cm)
35–65 lb (16–29 kg)

Description This dog is medium-sized with a lean, muscular body and a coarse coat. The coat color and pattern are varied, but red merle, blue merle, red, or black are common. The tail is either very short or missing.

Temperament The Australian shepherd is intelligent, easily trained, obedient, and responsive.

Grooming The coat needs very little attention. Brush occasionally and bathe only when necessary.

Exercise and feeding This dog needs plenty of vigorous exercise. There are no special feeding requirements.

Health problems A hardy breed, this dog may suffer from hip dysplasia, eye problems, and sunburn and scarring of the nose ("collie nose"). It is also sensitive to some heartworm preventatives. Merles are prone to deafness.

Independent, good-natured, energetic

 Regular brushing

 Regular, moderate

 Adapts well to urban living, but needs plenty of exercise

 Good watchdog

♂ Male
21–24 in (53–61 cm)
45–65 lb (20–29 kg)

♀ Female
20–23 in (51–58 cm)
40–60 lb (18–27 kg)

Description There are two types of collie: the rough collie and the smooth collie. These are identical except for the length of the coat, which comes in sable, blue merle, and tricolor. Its collar, chest, feet, and tail tip are white.

Temperament A very sociable dog, it is good with children, but can be high-strung and aloof with strangers. It is smart and easy to train, but can be a terrible barker.

Grooming A thorough weekly brushing will keep the double coat in good shape. Bathe as necessary.

Exercise and feeding The collie needs plenty of daily exercise. There are no special feeding requirements.

Health problems It is subject to epilepsy, hip dysplasia, skin and eye problems, and severe sunburn and scarring of the nose. It is sensitive to some heartworm preventatives.

Rough collie

306 Shetland sheepdog

Obedient, intelligent, loving

Regular brushing

Regular, moderate

Ideal for apartment living,
but needs plenty of exercise

Good watchdog

♂ Male
13–15 in (33–38 cm)
14–18 lb (6–8 kg)

♀ Female
12–14 in (30–36 cm)
12–16 lb (5–7 kg)

Description Strong and lightly built, this dog has a long, shaggy coat that mostly comes in sable, blue merle, and tricolor. It also comes in black with white or tan.

Temperament The sensitive Sheltie is easy to train, but may be shy or nervous, and is better suited to older children. Excessive barking may be a problem.

Grooming Regular brushing and removal of mats is important. The dense undercoat sheds heavily twice a year. Bathe or dry shampoo only when absolutely necessary.

Exercise and feeding This dog loves to play outdoors. It is prone to obesity, so avoid overfeeding it.

Health problems It is prone to von Willebrand's disease, epilepsy, "collie nose," and liver, heart, eye, and skin diseases. It is also sensitive to some heartworm preventatives.

308 German shepherd

 Fearless, devoted, intelligent

 Daily brushing

 Regular, vigorous

 Adapts well to urban living, but needs plenty of space

Outstanding watchdog

♂ Male
24–26 in (61–66 cm)
75–95 lb (34–43 kg)

♀ Female
22–24 in (56–61 cm)
70–90 lb (32–41 kg)

Description This dog has a dense double coat that mostly comes in black with tan, fawn, or gray markings.

Temperament A confident dog, this breed is often aggressive to other dogs and requires firm, kind, and consistent handling from a strong, experienced adult.

Grooming Daily grooming is necessary, especially during molting periods. Bathe or dry shampoo only when necessary.

Exercise and feeding This dog revels in strenuous activity and needs daily exercise or it will become destructive. Feed it two or three small meals a day.

Health problems It suffers from von Willebrand's disease, hip and elbow dysplasia, diabetes, epilepsy, spinal paralysis, inflammatory bowel disease, bloat, and skin, heart, and eye ailments. It may develop chronic diarrhea.

Border collie

 Intelligent, cooperative, joyful

 Regular brushing

 Regular, vigorous

 Adapts to urban living, but needs plenty of space and exercise

 Good watchdog

♂ Male
18–21 in (46–53 cm)
30–45 lb (14–20 kg)

♀ Female
17–20 in (43–51 cm)
27–42 lb (12–19 kg)

Description This well-proportioned dog has a double coat that comes mainly in black with white, but tricolored with tan and blue merle with white markings are also seen.

Temperament Eager to please, the border collie makes a wonderful pet, especially in homes with children. It is easily trained. However, it may bark excessively and be scrappy and jealous with other dogs.

Grooming Regular grooming is desirable, especially when the coat is molting. Bathe or dry shampoo when necessary.

Exercise and feeding This athletic dog thrives on hard work and play, and will become destructive when bored. There are no special feeding requirements.

Health problems Generally hardy, this breed is subject to some joint problems and genetic eye diseases.

| Bearded collie

 Brave, responsive, playful

 Daily brushing

 Regular, vigorous

 Adapts well to urban living, but needs plenty of exercise

 Good watchdog

♂ Male
21–22 in (53–56 cm)
45–55 lb (20–25 kg)

♀ Female
20–21 in (51–53 cm)
40–50 lb (18–23 kg)

Description The bearded collie has a shorter muzzle than other collies. The harsh coat comes in gray, red, slate, black, brown, and fawn, with or without white markings. It has a silky beard and abundant feathering (fringing).

Temperament This breed is intelligent, friendly, and loves children, but because of its size and herding instinct, it may scare a small child.

Grooming Daily brushing is vital to prevent matting. Also, the coat can be clipped every two months. Bathe or dry shampoo when necessary.

Exercise and feeding This is an active dog that needs lots of exercise. There are no special feeding requirements.

Health problems It is generally healthy, although hip dysplasia and eye defects occasionally occur.

Acknowledgments

PHOTOGRAPHIC CREDITS
Key t=top; l=left; r=right; tl=top left; tc=top center; tr=top right; cl=center left; c=center; cr=center right; b=bottom; bl=bottom left; bc=bottom center; br=bottom right.

APL=Australian Picture Library; APL/CBT=Australian Picture Library/Corbis; APL/MP=Australian Picture Library/Minden Pictures; AUS=Auscape International; COR=Corel Corp.; FHP=foxhillphoto; GI=Getty Images; PD=Photodisc.

All photographs by Stuart Bowey/Ad-Libitum (© Weldon Owen Pty Ltd) except:

2c Ariel Skelley/APL/CBT; 5c APL/CBT; 6c APL/CBT; 8c GI; 10l GI; 12bl Jean-Paul Ferrero; 14c APL/MP; 22l APL/CBT; 27l APL/CBT; 30tl COR; 31c APL/MP; 34l APL; 38c GI; 41l APL/CBT; 45c Eyewire; 46l GI; 55l APL/CBT; 57c APL/CBT; 59br APL/CBT; 64l APL/CBT; 69c APL/CBT; 72l GI; 74bl PD; 75c COR; 88l GI; 91c APL/CBT; 92c APL/CBT; 99c Karin Bridge;

103c APL/CBT; 109l GI; 111c FHP; 114l APL/MP; 116cr PD; 130c APL/CBT; 134l APL/CBT; 140l GI; 147tl FHP; 150l APL/CBT; 174c GI; 178l GI; 196c APL/CBT; 210c APL/CBT; 236l APL/CBT; 256l APL/CBT; 278l APL/CBT; 298l APL/CBT.

ILLUSTRATION CREDITS
Virginia Gray; Janet Jones; Iain McKellar; Chris Wilson.

INDEX
Puddingburn Publishing Services

CONSULTANT EDITOR
Dr. Paul McGreevy is a Senior Lecturer for the Faculty of Veterinary Science at the University of Sydney, Australia, and is recognized by the Royal College of Veterinary Surgeons as a specialist in Veterinary Behavioral Medicine. He is the author of three books on animal behavior and the editor of nine previous pet care titles.